Gadfly in Russia

Gadfly in Russia

Alan Sillitoe

BOOKS

First published in Great Britain in 2007 by JR Books,
10 Greenland Street, London NW1 9ND
www.jrbooks.com

A catalogue record for this book is available from the British
Library.

ISBN 978 1 906217 12 9

1 3 5 7 9 10 8 6 4 2

Typeset by SX Composing DTP, Rayleigh, Essex
Printed and bound in Great Britain by Cromwell Press, Trowbridge, Wiltshire.

Contents

Part One

Motoring There
1967

The only essay I remember writing at school was about the German advance into Russia during the Second World War. After mentioning the Napoleonic Campaign of 1812 I said that the aim of the current offensive in the Ukraine was to acquire the oil wells in the Caucasus, to fuel the Nazi economy. I was thirteen, but had probably taken most of it from a newspaper.

The first topographical map I owned was sent from Stanford's to me in Nottingham, a sheet covering the Stalingrad region, on which to follow the fighting. It cost two shillings and three pence, and came rolled in a cardboard tube. I still have it.

Fascination with Russia remained, even after the final victories. In 1963 I stayed a month in the country, and wrote a book called *Road to Volgograd*. In the summer of 1967, impelled to get away from my writing for a while, I sent a letter to Oksana Krugerskaya in Moscow, whom I'd met on the prior trip:

Having finished a novel, and with time to spare, I would like to visit Russia again. I'll drive there in my own car through Finland, and as for the itinerary, let's say a couple of days in Leningrad, and the same for Moscow. Then I'll go to Kiev and Chernovtsy, and out into Rumania. This will mean about two weeks in the USSR, so would it be possible to collect enough royalties from the translation of

Key to the Door to pay my hotel bills? Please cable me if this can be done, then I'll make bookings.

In accepting the plan Oksana said I would be met in Leningrad by a graduate of English from Moscow University called George Andjaparidze, who would stay with me all the way to the Rumanian frontier. I didn't like the idea, preferring to motor on my own. Perhaps it would be possible to avoid his company soon after my arrival.

As it turned out I was to know him for most of my life. His adventures with me, and misadventures with others, will be related in their place.

Monday, 12 June 1967
It wasn't the biggest of cars, being fifteen feet from snout to stern, but would more than do. Everything necessary for the journey was stowed on board. My son, five-year-old David, unhappy at seeing me go, watched from the top of the steps, old enough to imagine that some catastrophe might stop me coming back. He was right to wonder, since there were five thousand miles to cover, all plotted and mapped.

Why was I going? He couldn't or wouldn't articulate. It wasn't his fault, but he might have thought so in the confusing tunnels of his mind, as he brought another box by way of help. A child senses a betrayal of custody when you leave home for no obvious reason. Voluntary absence was an insoluble puzzle to him, even though I promised a cargo of presents from the retail outlets of Soviet Muscovy. Doubling a month's spending money into his warm palm, I broke free, and left him standing by the door. A last goodbye to my wife Ruth, and I was off.

All paperwork was done, a litany that set the heart racing:

visas, international driving licence, passport, car insurance, currencies and travellers' cheques, were in my wallet. The car had been fully serviced, even the brakes relined. At the garage the manager had sold me a box of spares, including, he said, all possible bulbs and fuses. He guided me out on to the street calling: 'You should have no trouble at all,' something I'd heard too many times to feel complacent.

The boxy dark blue Peugeot Estate made a northeasterly vector of escape. Too long where I no longer wanted to be had been no good for the heart. *A Tree on Fire* had taken much of the mind, as is the way with a novel, and was now with the publisher, but I still felt that my present venture was self-indulgence.

The gypsy in me surfaced on sounding the klaxon and showing a smile at green traffic lights, waving at other drivers and getting daggers back at my supposed high spirits. At times the sense of freedom faded, leaving only loneliness and deprivation. I had the urge to turn back, but pressed on across the Thames.

Wanting to get more quickly out of the country I cruised the outer lane at seventy, until a huge black wagon blocked the way ahead, and for no apparent reason braked. My heart fluttered like a sparrow's at the notion of a tangled wreck, but the Peugeot fitted into a leftward gap between another car and the municipal dustwagon. Life saved, the blue sky blessed me on towards Harwich.

I'd always wanted to get away from England, took every opportunity. Loving the place, I didn't often like it. Such an errant traveller was untrustworthy, liable at any moment to desert family or friends, but however much the tight-lipped stay-at-homes preferred it here, I paid no mindless homage to the cosy fixed customs of a particular piece of earth, and revelled in the fevered acts of departure, seeming only alive at the wheel of a car. Perhaps the zest for travel was a desire to find a spot that would provide tranquillity until death. No such place. The quest would be hopeless. If I thought that way I wouldn't drive a mile, never mind five thousand.

I telephoned from the quayside, and when David came on he sounded more grown up at my departure, asking me to bring back 'painted things', such as Palekh and Fidoskino gew-gaw boxes with hand-coloured scenes from Russian fairy tales on their lids.

The car was stowed, and a cabin allotted. Farewells suggest one might never return and, superstitious as travellers inevitably are, I refused to consider the possibility. One could, after all, be killed in an accident a mile from where one lived. Lunatic Hamlets shipped between Denmark and England must make up a good share of the two-way traffic.

Instead of giving a sardonic wave to the nondescript marshes of Essex I sat for dinner in the Danish ship that was called *England*. The food was as good as London fare was vile. At my table a paunchy grey-haired businessman of about fifty said he was on his way to Copenhagen and then Cologne in a Humber Imperial. He wasn't put out by my questions, and we went on to talk about the campaign of Israel against Syria, Egypt and Jordan, both of us sufficiently informed after reading the *Sunday Times* account. Judging by his interesting reappraisal of the conflict he must at one time have been a soldier.

In the cabin I listened on shortwave to an adaptation of *Mr Norris Changes Trains*. Then the news was read which, as the saying goes, went in one ear and out the other. On deck at half past ten waves beat along the ship's white flanks, the western horizon a deep pink above a wide band of green and blue. Venus, the first star of the evening, kept company with a sickle of moon.

Travelling alone was a form of deracination. Nothing seemed real, drifting through nowhere in my lit-up coffin of a cabin, one of the almost dead only to come fully alive on driving into Denmark. A vibrating of engines and the rush of water suggested that an unfathomably devious will had brought me to where I was.

Lights off, the ship made headway. From the radio again a voice said that one should not be afraid to die. I wasn't, thank you very much. Why should I be? If the earth had fallen on my foot, and left me lame – metaphorically speaking – I was nevertheless still able to walk. Snug in spirit, I switched off the light, wondering why I didn't much care about anyone or anything, because being en route for Russia filled me with optimism, and I fell asleep.

Tuesday, 13 June
A young marine engineer with a reddish beard was riding to New Zealand on a powered bicycle, and expected to reach Singapore in six months. Slender and of middle height, he wore a checked shirt and jeans, and I wished him good luck as he gazed towards land after breakfast. Travelling so light, he seemed set for privation, though I didn't doubt he would get to the Antipodes, sooner or later. On docking at Esbjerg his bike wouldn't start, so he pushed it ashore to find a mechanic.

The Peugeot shot from the quayside like a lion from its cage, as if smelling raw meat on the road ahead, and took me through the town on a well-scaped scenic highway. On the short ferry crossing between Nyborg and Korsør the deck entertainment system played Paul Robeson records, while over a coffee and pastry I checked the route – idly, for I needn't have done – given by the AA. Petrol pumps, places with hotels, and interesting cultural sites were indicated, though I also had Baedeker's more or less up-to-date *Touring Guide to Scandinavia* in the glove box for more detailed information.

At Elsinore by six o'clock, I had crossed Denmark in five hours, but what was the hurry? Don't bother to tell me, I told myself. There was ample time to do the thousand miles to Leningrad, and meet George Andjaparidze.

The route had been familiar from two years before, when with Ruth and David we had gone through Elsinore on our way to Koli in Karelian Finland. At Hamlet Town we had strolled by the castle shore hoping to find the swan moat where Ophelia perished.

Rain came for a while in Sweden, and every sensible motorist showed headlights. I followed their example. The forest to either side, called *skog* and pronounced 'shoe', was dense and dark. Last time we stopped for a picnic, only to flee from meat-eating flies as big as overripe blackberries, and their fighter escorts of virulent mosquitoes.

By dusk, which would last nearly all night, I staggered mile-drunk into a small hotel at Lagan, glad to find a room. Walking the street before an evening meal I noted the Swedish fondness for flagpoles, each garden flying a proud banner of blue and yellow. Perhaps a national day was coming up, or the poles were thought of as totems or symbolic trees, seasoned to death and stripped of bark and branches, so many billion matches lost to the world. The first Swedish word I learned was *tändsticka*, the matches to buy in Malaya because all local boxes fell to pieces as soon as you picked them up.

The only other people in the restaurant were a man and a little girl supping at the next table. No word was spoken by either. The girl, ten or eleven years old, had long slightly curled dark hair, and lived in her own silence, yet dominated it by the coolness of her expression. The father – or uncle, or guardian, it was hard to say – wore an open-necked shirt and unpressed jacket, and needed a shave, though was clean. The waitress joked with him, for the child's sake I thought, but he continued scooping at his soup as if no one else was in the room, unaware of her attractive milkmaid stance. She went away, but tried again to get some spark from him during cheerful deliveries of further courses.

It was hard to imagine the girl was his daughter, with her formed and sensitive features, where his were nondescript in the extreme. His grey-blue eyes looked vacantly around for a moment, then saw nothing but his place and bottle of beer, the spirit behind his fragmented face unwilling to assert itself beyond indicating that he was either overwhelmed with unhappiness or simple fatigue. Perhaps he was divorced, and this was the only time of the week when the girl, being his daughter after all, could be taken out.

I finished my meal, and lit a stubby Danish cigar. He turned as the match caught fire. The one I offered was accepted with a smile, and he lit it with exaggerated gestures: 'Churchill!' he cried, blowing out enough smoke to conceal the girl's eyes. 'English?'

I admitted it, so he held the cigar as high over the table as his arm could reach. 'Bomb!' and brought it down at a tangent, fumes trailing from the end. 'Berlin!' he added, treating his plate to the same amount of drifting coverage. When the waitress cleared our places she was rapturous at seeing him drawn at last from his presumed fit of misery.

Wednesday, 14 June

The weather was good, so at two o'clock I snacked by the roadside, set my radio on the bonnet, and played out the aerial to get news loud and clear from London. My weakness for wireless sets of good looks and performance had cost over a hundred pounds in Imhoff's on Oxford Street, for I didn't care to be cut off in Russia or the Balkans with only the *Daily Worker* as my bedside informant. Not that I listened while driving, preferring as much silence as possible. I never find engine noise unpleasant, however, having spent much of my youth in the noise of a factory, and since been little-boyishly fascinated by the machinery of aeroplanes, ships, trains (and cars) or the insides of shortwave radios.

I was going through Sweden as speedily as was safe, turning out miles like nuts and bolts on a capstan lathe during a factory's bull week before Christmas, yet thinking to come back one day and see the country as properly as it deserved, which I always tell myself while travelling. After 400 kilometres I broke through to the Baltic, and reached Trosa by three o'clock, booking into the same hotel as two years ago and by coincidence being given the room David had slept in.

Trosa was a quiet place off the main road, a collection of neat wooden houses mostly closed and perhaps waiting for the celebrations of Midsummer's Eve. They backed on to the canal, with a car or sailing dinghy (or both) nearby, and pyramids of logs for winter weekends. I could only hope the pyromaniacs in Sweden were under strict surveillance.

The coastline was indistinct, impossible to tell where land ended because of so many small islands in the way, but high-chested swans floated on their birthright of water, savouring the soft Baltic rain starting to fall.

Paul Robeson's sonorous and melancholy voice mellowing out 'Old Man River' from the hotel speaker suggested that such entertainment had followed me from Denmark, though I supposed I might hear him again in Russia. The world outside seemed a bigger and more mysterious place during rain, and Robeson's familiar songs brought back childhood, and made me wonder why I was in a hotel hundreds of miles from where I lived. It generally took three full days to get used to being on the road.

I refused to question why I was on earth. I'd never got into the habit, having realised how pointless it was. Let rain fall and gloom gather. I was going to where I would look for what could not be found, before settling for the enjoyment of travelling for its own sake. Paul Robeson sang as an exile who could never go home again, a man whose home is wherever he happens to be.

I stayed at my late meal till the dining room was nearly empty. The waitress all along had given me intense appraisals, even when serving at other tables, as if half recognising me from somewhere, and wanting to talk and find out more. She was thirty or so, wore slacks and an army style jacket over a white shirt. Short fair hair framed a weary prematurely lined face, as if she'd had a long day, or between lunch and dinner had suffered a fraught and exhausting time with her lover. Certainly her grey eyes shone with curiosity as she stood by my table for payment. Her quick smile showed her as fundamentally shy, as if knowing that should we not talk now we never would, and so lose each other for ever. But I was exhausted after so much time at the wheel, and we said not a word – another photograph into the memory box.

Thursday, 15 June

After a bout of heavy rain the sun came out. I stopped in a village to telegraph my publisher in Finland, to say I'd be calling on him the following morning.

I lost my way in the intricate (for me) approaches to Stockholm, though on the former trip there had been no problem. The previous night I'd looked hard at the town plan to check the route but, being exhilarated, I drove too fast and took wrong turnings. In the northern suburbs I got out and walked to a crossroads, read the street signs, and fixed my position. The white ship to Finland was waiting at the landing stage.

I watched the Peugeot lifted by a crane, its mudstained underbelly revealed, hoping the body wouldn't bend like the long new car I once saw being similarly hauled on to the Majorca boat from the quayside of Barcelona. Its American owner watched, curious yet confident, but as the vehicle began its ascent, firmly hooked at all four corners, it began bending before our eyes, and his aspect changed to one that seemed brought on by seasickness. The clearly visible man at the crane grinned as if telling himself that whatever was happening couldn't be his fault.

The higher the car went the more out of place the chassis became. The American was fond of his car, as who wouldn't be, for he'd had it shipped from the United States, so far unscathed. I heard it bending, as did others, and we scattered from its vicinity like ants from vinegar. I later learned that an insurance company paid for the somewhat buckled vehicle, Spanish mechanics at that time having a reputation for doing what many considered impossible.

Nowadays one drives directly into the hold of boats from Barcelona, but not on the *Allotar* plying between Stockholm and Helsinki, though my car and a few others were stowed without damage.

Propellors pulverised the water. The gap between boat and quay was soon already too wide for those to jump who might change their minds about leaving. Sweden was out of touch, yet still not out of mind as I muttered thank you for my fair passage through. But no land could hold me when another was in the offing. For eighteen shipboard hours I could rest without being bored.

Our boat took long to reach open sea, the Scandinavian summer spreading heat over light blue water of the archipelago. Rocky islets with a tree or two were sprinkled to port and starboard, each with its summerhouse, landing stage, speed boat, and sunbathers now and again observed through my Barr and Stroud binoculars, bringing to mind Stig Dagerman's novel *A Burnt Child*, in which the seduction of the hero by his father's mistress takes place on one such island.

In the cafeteria-saloon a tall well-built man in suit and loosened tie, a shamanic grin on his blue-eyed sweating face, played a large electric accordian loud enough to loosen the rivets. The mostly middle aged who danced to his tune enjoyed the high pagan music of Swedish midsummer madness. A man who came exhausted (momentarily) from the throng explained that they belonged to a coach party of Finns who had been touring Sweden – a country they seemed in no way sad to leave.

As far as possible from the noise I drank coffee, and talked to a black man of twenty-five who sipped Coca-Cola. He told me – as well as his age – that he was going to live in Finland. He'd spent some years in Sweden but decided that it had no soul. He'd heard that Finland was more complicated in that respect.

I told him I didn't agree with his views on Sweden, and in any case people were more or less the same everywhere. He'd become fed up and wanted a change. 'Well,' he said, 'I know what I'm talking about. I lived five years in Sweden, where I earned a living teaching English. I hope to do the same in Helsinki.' I wished him luck.

The estuary widened, islands and shoreline more distant, sun burning but wind flapping across the boat on its way through calm water. To be cut off from the past seemed the purest state of contentment, though an antisocial zone of grace that sociologists deplore and psychiatrists strive to rob one of.

A sense of emptiness spun me down into a cul-de-sac, while the drug of the pure sky spurred me to annoyance at the plodding rate of the boat. I was eager to be back on land and driving east, with the devil behind and new scenery in front, to rejuvenate the soul yet not blacken the heart, a healing process, as I sat on deck in the sun and planned (and imagined) one motoring expedition after another, taking enough zigzags across the map to last a lifetime, and never thinking to go home again.

The ship rocked slightly and began to turn as I totted up the distances between Kiev and Karaganda, Paris and Peking, Sofia and Saigon, Cape Town and Komsomolsk-on-the-Amur. What trips, Pip! The longest highways in the world would one day be possible by Peugeot and Opel, Ford and Volvo, their drivers without passports and visas. The odd few might die of thirst in desert or salt marsh while travelling from Tiflis to Astrakhan, but what the hell!

I went to my second-class cabin for a change of handkerchief, and found a man of great corpulency packed into the top bunk, snoring louder than the engines. Jacket and shirt collar hung by the sink, shoes on the floor tripped me, and the air was so heavy with alcohol fumes I wouldn't have dared light a match, unless there was time for me to reach a lifeboat. He was a child of heaven so drunk I wondered why he had put himself to the effort of achieving the higher place instead of wedging his parcel shape into the bottom one. Perhaps he'd imagined he was already in it, and the sea had been a bit rough in throwing him so high.

White birds chipped at the masts, and the music went on as if providing power for the boat to steer by. I asked a tall dark girl with large eyes and white skin where she had come from and where she was going. Set apart from everyone, she looked suspicious, as if I might be an evil traveller only wanting to get her into my cabin. On such a crowded boat, for God's sake?

As I talked, obviously without malign intent, she told me she was going home after serving five years in a mission station on the Greenland coast, working as a printer of Eskimo newspapers. We discussed the explorer and anthropologist Rasmussen, whose book I had recently read at Ted Hughes's place in Devon, but soon we had no more to say, locked too deeply in our separate musings for further connection to be made. Perhaps she had not seen her boyfriend since going to Greenland, and was on her way back to marry him. He would be on the quay to meet her in the morning, and the prospect of domestic bliss had even now lost any attraction for her. The thoughts she wanted to be alone with at the moment seemed more comforting than those a husband would be able to tolerate.

Threading the Åland Islands was something I had done before, but being alone gave a different state of mind, more prosaic and free. The deep blue sea rippled, and the horizon became a rose-coloured band rising to orange and yellow, the faint green above dissolving into steeliness, then a universal door holding back real darkness.

At midnight the boat steadily ploughed, a buoy so close to the porthole I could almost have put out an arm and touched it. The manic accordian still played, and probably would till morning.

Night wouldn't come no matter how long I waited. The sun just above grey water watched the boat go by, and I couldn't sleep under its bland stare, though a white fluorescent sickle of moon eventually persuaded me into a sort of unconsciousness, and at one o'clock I got into bed hoping that the heavy man above wouldn't wake before breakfast. He lay in an oblivion that knew neither sun nor moon.

Friday, 16 June

I was too knocked up after the disturbed night to take in the impressive approach to Helsinki, so can't describe it. As the boat docked a band on the quay played to receive our load of tourists who had kept up their high-stepping for all of the voyage back to their homeland. To similar tunes they filed down the gangway waving and laughing at waiting friends, a wall of noise loud enough for the ship to lean against, and so vibrating the eardrums that I too began to feel part of the welcome.

I stood on the quayside for a few minutes before the car descended, meanwhile studying a plan of the city. A girl from one of the oil companies asked if I needed any motoring information. Like an angel of light, though with dark hair (which maybe all angels have) she handed out maps and pamphlets. I'd noticed in Stockholm that the left and right blinkers of the Peugeot were not flashing when switched on to turn or overtake, a serious matter driving on the right side of the road and with the car seat in the English position. To lessen the possibility of accidents it had to be seen to as soon as possible, so I asked the young woman the name of the nearest Peugeot garage and what street it was on. She explained everything with the utmost economy of sweetness, before moving on to another dazed motorist.

Navigating more by intuition and luck I followed the cobbled boulevard and found the garage on Arkadiankatu. The supervisor looked at the bulbs and fuses bought in London and said none were of the type to solve the problem, but he had the necessary parts and would have the job done in a couple of hours.

The Otava Publishing Company was a mere half mile away. I was shown into the opulent office of the managing director, Mr Erkii Reenpaa, a tall slim man in his forties, formally dressed (unlike myself) as a person of status, his somewhat draculous aspect belied by a glittery-eyed sense of humour.

Talking about my onward travels he said, as we smoked our cigars, that his firm was about to produce a complete guide to the Intourist motor routes currently open in the Soviet Union. The problem was that no detailed maps of the country were available.

From my briefcase I showed the elaborate tracings made of the road from Leningrad to Moscow and Kiev, on the scale of eight miles to an inch, based on British War Office maps and printed by the Royal Engineers. I had inked in villages, spot heights and water features, as well as additions from a few Russian maps. Also marked was the latest AA and Intourist information, indicating petrol pumps, hotels and service stations (few and far between) along the way. I had also altered those placenames which once had 'Stalin' in them. Spread out as well were the larger scale Austrian survey maps of southwest Russia between Kiev and Rumania which, though out of date, would still be useful. Other navigation equipment, I told him, included a prismatic compass readable to one degree, binoculars, and my shortwave radio receiver.

He was too much of a Finn – and a gentleman – to raise his hands in shock at my irresponsible naïvety, yet real concern came into his voice. I ought not, he said, to let the Soviet customs officers see such detailed maps. If found they would certainly be confiscated, and even supposing they still let you in you would be under surveillance for the whole of your stay. And if you do manage to smuggle them through don't flaunt them too readily by the roadside. As for the radio you must have it marked in your passport at the frontier, otherwise there'll be a fuss when you try to take it out.

I had spent many enjoyable and therapeutic hours making those maps, so they would certainly be used, to get the most out of my trip. I didn't after all want to lose my way. An enticing stretch of scenery or piece of architecture would have to be marked so that I would remember exactly where it had been. In any case, I told him, I never travelled without the best maps, and as for spying over the fair land of secretive Mother Russia, weren't United States satellites already photographing every building and footpath, and from them constructing maps that would make mine look as accurate as a seaman's chart in the fifteenth century?

He smiled indulgently at my supposed recklessness, then invited me to his house for dinner, adding that I could spend the night as well. When I told him that my last stop in Finland would be at Virolahti, just before the Russian frontier, he picked up the telephone and spoke to a friend who was a bookseller in that village. It was arranged that I would lodge overnight at the man's summerhouse on the shore of the Gulf.

'And if you'd like a sauna' – he smiled on my saying I would – 'you'll get a good one there.'

Back at the garage I was told by the fair and buxom receptionist that all the car lights had been checked and were now in working order. 'Are you going to the Arctic Circle?' she asked.

'No. I'm going to Russia.'

'In that case you must buy a spare set of windscreen wipers, because those you have at the moment are sure to disappear if you leave your car unguarded even for five minutes in that country. It happens to everyone.'

I already knew there were plenty of thieves in Moscow, having lost an expensive fountain pen from a pickpocket on a previous visit. I'd always assumed stealing to have some legitimacy if in need of bread to eat – well, maybe as long as it wasn't from me. Pilfering was a fact of life that had to be guarded against, such as never walking around with a wallet showing from your back pocket. You can't relax for a moment, and though Karl Marx had said that 'property was theft' I supposed he would have squealed like a stuck pig if he'd gone into a shop and found his money missing when he came to pay at the till.

Since I seemed liable to lose my windscreen wipers in Russia I took the woman's advice and bought an extra set. With vigilance they might not be stolen, so the spare ones would no doubt go to rust in the back of the car. In general I trusted my neighbour while at the same time regarding everyone as potentially light fingered. Even so, on hearing that 'all men are brothers' my instinct is to take to the hills with a quantity of tobacco and a rifle.

I browsed in Stockman's department store, from one treasure

hall to the next, but wasn't tempted to buy anything among the crowds of silent jostlers. Finding it too hot to stay indoors I headed twenty miles out of the city, forking on to a track from the main road and going through fields and patches of forest. I got out of the car at an isolated place, to lie down and let the sky be my blanket. No sounds except from birds in pine and birch trees, I couldn't nevertheless do justice to the advantage and fall asleep. I smoked, wrote notes and letters, making myself as much at home as possible. I read more of a novel by Väinö Linna called *The Unknown Soldier,* one of the best war novels I'd so far come across, describing the fight of the Finnish army against the overwhelming Russians during the Winter War of 1939–40. I sacrificed sleep to go on with it, yet wondered what I would do when it was finished. I could of course start the Everyman two volumes of *The Kalevala,* which would certainly keep me going.

On the way back to Helsinki the sideblinkers packed up again. Driving on the motorway and even unable to use hand signals was a nightmare, for I was now on the unfamiliar right side of the road as well. I had to cut my speed and take extra care, while cursing those at the garage as potential murderers.

Saturday, 17 June
My first stop was at the Peugeot establishment, where I gave a few black looks and asked them to fix the bloody blinkers, this time for keeps. For all their silence they had been in some way incompetent, and I stood over the mechanic during the half hour's work and final testing, till he assured me I would have no further trouble.

With most of the fine day to drive only 200 kilometres I pulled up for a couple of young men by the roadside who gave the autostop sign. They knew some English, and in chatting told me they were amateur long distance runners. Realising I was English they expressed great admiration for the champion Gordon Pirie.

Two years previously, in the same month almost to the day, with Ruth and David in the car, I was voyaging northeast towards Karelia in very different weather. Veils of rain slicked from low cloud, our plucky Austin A40 Countryman ploughing through with little trouble. At a café between road and lake for coffee and cakes , and milk for three-year-old David, I pushed a few coins into a juke box to amuse him with the latest Finnish top of the pops. A man took a liking to him – as who would not? – and carried him out to the water's edge, where he broke up a couple of sweet buns for what looked like four thousand fishes which, to David's delight, poked their snouts above the water to snap them up.

The weather grew worse for us beyond Lappeenranta, and the unpaved road, marked red on the map, which we had almost to ourselves, widened to a hundred yards of slippery ox-blood mud. Rain cut visibility until we seemed to be swaying along underwater, wind blasting from the Soviet border to the east. After a hundred miles of such piloting I turned northwest for Savonlinna, and a hotel in which the kindly Mr Reenpaa had booked a room for us. I moored the car by the pavement about midnight, and a band with singer performed in the almost empty dining room, where we were too exhausted to take in anything but soup.

Next day in better weather we backtracked to Punkaharju for a sauna at the Hotel Finlandia. Before entering the steam room the resident old lady in attendance loofered our naked bodies from top to bottom. Her job was to keep the place clean, stoke the stove and provide towels – as well as bundles of birch twigs.

We decided to introduce David to the same hot mill, on the assumption that it would be fun, good for his body and soul, and an experience to remember, but the washing and splashing and steaming and beating scared him, and he escaped outside to play in the sand, watched over by the woman.

After the ordeal I ran along the wooden jetty and went down like a naked arrow into the water, revitalised for further travelling, then through the trees for lemon tea in the hotel lounge.

Back to the future, I drove with pipe and cigar smoke drifting from four open windows. An enormous lorry, going almost as fast as myself, was there for overtaking on the empty treelined road. I glanced at the side mirrors, gauged his speed, pressed on the blinkers now fully operating, swung out, dropped gear on drawing level, and shot by with a roar. I then upped the gears to get well ahead, and settled my speed at just over seventy.

Such travelling should have brought out the supposedly eternal faculties of a writer – memory, observation, and imagination – but they weren't apparent, my brain being empty on driving alone through new territory and having to use all practical sense to stay alive.

By now a long way from London I thought it best not to wonder how far there was still to go before edging homewards. I was a nonentity at his machine on a conveyor belt of road, churning out miles, only interested in how many I would clock up that day. People close to me had drifted away, for the moment anyway. No one was necessary to define my identity or place, which was why I had set out on the road. It was an agreeable state, that of a hermit perhaps, or misanthrope, alone at last and with few thoughts straying in.

At Hamina I went into the bus station café for lunch, and though people watched from close by I wasn't inclined to get into conversation. I ate the meal hurriedly and left, glad to get to Virolahti where Pekko Tulkki was to meet me on his way back from a wedding. His bookshop was closed until that time, so I sat in a café writing postcards to Ruth and David, and to Ted Hughes and David Storey. I went through my address book to see who else I could send one to. No one in the place spoke English, and for the first time I used the phrase list from Baedeker, though the pronunciation must have mystified my words. But some got through when buying stamps from the post office later. The girls behind the bar talked slyly and in whispers, so that even if I'd known a fair amount of their language it would have been impossible to understand them. The situation reminded me of that in Ingmar Bergman's film *The Silence*.

Pekko Tulkki was about fifty, neat, fair, balding, and amiable, his gnome-like Finnish eyes seeming to reflect the lakes and forests of his fascinating country. I recalled giving a lift to a man during our time in Karelia, who stood by the road far from house or village. Sparse woods and marsh went into infinity, the summery sky about to let down rain. He was slight of build, wore shirt, trousers, and local shoes like exotic carpet slippers. He gave no indication of wanting to hitchhike, but when I stopped he climbed in without a word and sat with David in the back. There was no common language except for him to take in where we had come from that day, and recognise the name of Koli on Lake Pielinen where we were going. I couldn't be sure how much the placenames meant to him, yet he was keen on getting into communication. He had short incredibly white hair, and skin corked by the sun. His pale eyes glistened like opals, restless yet deep and piercing when he spoke. Though his skin was wrinkled he seemed no more than forty, and filled the car with the aura of a troll, or ghost, smiling with thin narrow lips.

David, an infallible litmus paper, was happy to be sitting by him as I drove along the unpaved road, till after about thirty kilometres he made signs that we were where he wanted to be. We also got out of the car and, being hungry, I jabbed a finger at my mouth to find out whether he cared for anything to eat, with a further sign that he was welcome to join us. He declined, but asked for pencil and paper, so I passed the current map on whose corner he wrote with some effort the shaky letters of his name: Pektti Hannolau – as far as I could make out. He wanted our names in return, so I put them down in block capitals using paper he could take away. After shaking hands we left him by the roadside, his arm lifted in farewell.

Pekko at Virolahti told me to follow his car, and led me at great speed along a smooth and narrow track through the forest. Then came bumps and curves that almost threw me into the trees as I tried not to lose sight of him. He was an architect and bookseller, who had designed and built a wooden summer-house on an inlet of the Gulf of Finland. The Russian shore, a thousand yards across the water, was marked by watchtowers above the tree tops. Scanning them with binoculars I had no doubt that, guarding their prison or paradise, they were likewise observing me. The local Finns were long used to the situation, Pekko said, and no one on their side anyway was at all nervous. I found it strange that if Russia was a prison people were prevented from leaving, and a paradise others were barred from entering, there were no queues on either side of the frontier.

The sauna hut was set on rocks a few yards from the water.

We changed after supper, Pekko bronzed and me chalkish white. The stove well lit, he threw cold water on to scorching stones, steam coiling till sweat ran from my scalp, out of cuticles and eyeballs, every nook and bend of flesh.

Swishing birch twigs disturbed the air to bring some relief, and if the pleasant smell was to be the last on earth then so be it. He glanced at the thermometer, decided it read too low, and splashed another ladle of water on to the stones, clouds billowing till I couldn't see anything, wondering where the door was in case of a blackout.

'All right?'

'Fine,' I said.

Another dollop of water took away the last vodka drunk at supper. Steam was eating me up. Having shed as much moisture as could possibly be in me, or so I thought, I was ready to wave the white flag. Birch leaves no longer helped, since the water they rested in between bouts, too warm to encourage circulation, burned on impact with the skin. I managed to control my breathing when lungs seemed about to pop like paper bags. Mr Reenpaa's mischievous smile on telling me I would be sure to get a good sauna in Virolahti came back.

Pekko considered we had more liquid (and dirt) to lose. I climbed up on to the planks to lie down, but it was better to keep moving, so I went back to the floor as another billow of volcanic heat reminded me of cleaning the flues of a factory boiler system as a boy of fourteen, crawling along narrow tunnels to spade away heaps of still hot clinker and soot.

When by common consent Pekko opened the door I ran for the lake as if death was behind me, swimming through pink-reflecting bars of the setting sun.

He took me and his lovely daughter by motorboat around the

darkening bay, careful to avoid going too far and risking a few bullets from the Russians. Pale smoke from other sauna chimneys drifted along the shore. Pekko greeted the local police chief who stood on a jetty fresh from his own bath, an immensely powerful man in his middle thirties, the space between hair and eyes narrow, but the smile wide. He looked cleaner than anyone I'd ever seen.

I sat by the shore in the gloaming, not a breath of wind, but my lighter flame bent at such an angle I assumed the fuel was running out. At half past ten numerous birds throated their calls, sometimes in chorus. Hard to believe I was alive. Tiredness turned everything into a dream. Love was lacking, and cuckoos instead of nightingales sang for much of the night.

Sunday, 18 June
Waterloo Day, the sixth out of London. Pekko came to the frontier village of Vaalima, to have coffee and say goodbye. The road beyond the Finnish post was blocked by a control arm, as if the Flying Scotsman was expected to steam through any minute. A Soviet soldier stood by his sentry box, no other building in sight. Stirring music sounded from a loudspeaker at the top of a tall pole, a noise like the crashlanding of a stricken aircraft. After ten minutes the soldier picked up his field telephone and spoke into it. He listened, said yes a few times, and put it down.

I lit a cigar and looked at my map of the road to Leningrad. The day was warm, so I opened all windows. He lifted the telephone again, and motioned me along the treelined potholed road. After about a kilometre I saw the neat modern customs house, a hammer-and-sickle at half flutter, and another megaphonic instrument blared martial music.

Three cars were in front, Swedish, Finnish, and Australian. All doors were being opened and bonnets lifted. One was of the dormobile type and a customs man went inside to look in drawers and under beds, while another pulled seats forward to examine the upholstery.

I was motioned into the building to show my passport, and when its visa was checked the woman handed me a form several sheets long on which I was to state exactly how much foreign currency was in my wallet, of whatever denomination, whether in traveller's cheques or notes, then to declare the number of suitcases and pieces of smaller luggage, as well as camera, radio and field glasses. I followed a soldier out so that he could write the number of the engine and chassis, preliminaries which took about half an hour. It was eleven o'clock, by when I'd hoped to be beyond Viborg.

Soldiers were still going through the dormobile. One opened a jar of cold cream and put it to his nose. I looked forward to a laugh should he stir a finger inside for hidden jewels – but he thought better of it. Another swaddie paged his way through magazines looking for seditious reading matter, found none, but lingered a few moments over advertisements for women's underwear.

I strolled up and down. The people in the Swedish car, with fractious and impatient children, seemed about to go berserk at the delay. I sympathised, and gave the kids some chocolate. Getting into Russia by air had been easy compared to this. The Swedes laughed at my gesture of resignation. No cars had yet gone through.

My turn came. A clean-faced young soldier asked me to lift the tailgate. He opened my binocular case, looked at the radio, and saw the camera, all noted on the customs form, which he checked. Did I have a tape recorder? No, I told him. There was nothing I wanted to smuggle in, or much that I would care to take out, either, yet wondered what they hoped to find. I had a few presents for friends – a quantity of books (mostly my own) ballpoint pens, and some pop records.

Magazines were flipped through in a polite but thorough way. He'd been told to do a job, and was doing it, so I stayed calm and patient, knowing that wanting to get into Russia there was no point being otherwise. I understood a few phrases of their language but pretended to know only my own.

He asked why I had so many books, and who they were for. I said they were for giving away, which he didn't understand. Asking me to wait he went into the main building and a few minutes later came out with a stout woman wearing some kind of uniform who asked if I was intending to sell the books. When I said they were for friends she smiled and translated it to the soldier, who nevertheless continued lifting others into the light. I had Nagel's *Guide to the USSR*, 1965 and the *Guide Bleu Illustré Moscou-Leningrad* which were looked into as well.

I thought of my specially drawn cartographic efforts which, Mr Reenpaa had said, if found might be confiscated or get me sent back to Finland, a prospect by this time in no way alarming. They were ensconced in the pocket of a holdall resting against the inside of the car, and he diligently searched it but without moving it into an isolated position, thus not noticing the concealed zip.

Half an hour later I was free to go. Waving goodbye, I revved up in a cloud of smoke and took the road to Leningrad, having at last shaken my way free of so much bullshit. A few kilometres on, some boys of twelve or fourteen stood in the road and signalled me to stop. I was going too fast, but then three other boys flagged me down, and I decided to see what they wanted. As they closed in to look through the window I was careful to ensure no eager fingers made a grab for anything that took their fancy. Neat and cleanly dressed, they probably came from the nearby village of Torfyanovka. 'Hello,' I said in Russian, a greeting returned but without a smile. 'What do you want?' also in Russian.

I was eager to get the wheels rolling, having missed the drug of engine noise for so long at the frontier. There was no reason for hurry, but I was losing patience at their keen curiosity. They looked at every instrument and control in silence, hoping I supposed to discuss what they had seen later. Two more boys, as if too timid to approach the car, stood with long fishing poles by the trees, looking anxiously up and down the road.

I made a move to start the engine, when one of them asked for a cigarette. I told them in Russian that I didn't understand, but they made unmistakable signs of smoking, so I smiled and gave one each, and a couple more for the two keeping watch in case the police came and booted them away. They must have found it profitable, cadging a fag tax from each car that went through.

In Viborg, I changed my mind at having a big feed in the Intourist Hotel, because it would take at least an hour, and pulled up instead at a canteen sort of place near the bus station. The town seemed rundown, as was the building I ate in. Viborg had 80,000 Finnish inhabitants in 1945, and was called Viipuri, but rather than live under Soviet rule when the war ended every man woman and child left. The Russians took over a ghost town, and the main street even now had a certain frontier raffishness. Not much of it had been made in twenty years. Instead of Finnish neatness it was as if the Russians had built and colonised it from the beginning. The town's historical charm needed love and money to keep up, but the present inhabitants, not having been born there, didn't perhaps regard it as theirs, though I supposed that in a couple of generations they would no longer feel they had stolen it.

The canteen was almost empty because it was late for lunch, till a group of jolly workwomen came in from the bus station, queued for glasses of lemon tea, and sat at the scattered tables, reminding me of a British restaurant during the war.

The cash-desk woman flicked coloured beads left and right on her abacus frame, and charged fifty kopecks for my tray of ham, black bread, salad and a glass of prune juice – nothing hot, but I was well satisfied. About to light a cigar, I saw a no-smoking sign on the wall.

Even with windows open the thermometer in the car was close to a hundred. I passed better-kept dwellings on the outskirts. After a mile or so, after overtaking a horse and cart, I came to a narrow humpbacked bridge guarded by a soldier with rifle and bayonet. He waved me down, and I wondered what for. Had somebody telephoned from town and told him to stop me for an unspecified misdemeanour at the customs post?

Leaning his rifle against the wall he pulled a notebook from his tunic and, peering close, slowly copied the strange letters of the licence plate.

I got out and asked why he had stopped me, but my Russian wasn't good enough for him to understand. His gestures indicated that I must reverse the car and go back in the direction of Viborg.

I thought of pushing on over the bridge, but the consequences of a couple of live rounds put paid to that. Galled at the possibility of not reaching Leningrad, on a day that was already half gone, I saw myself answering questions for a fault I knew nothing about – a not unfamiliar situation, but only tolerable if it came at a time of my choosing.

Not paid to talk, he stabbed his rifle as a further sign that I should turn round. But why? And where to go? He posted himself again at the bridge, as I drove away wondering what would happen now.

I saw, on looking at the map, that I had missed the signpost for Leningrad, had made a left instead of a right fork, and taken a route not on the Intourist itinerary. The forbidden road ran northeast towards Lake Ladoga and Kamenogorsk, and I would happily have followed it – venture adventure – had the Gorshek soldier not pointed a bayonet at my guts.

A mere eighty kilometres since breakfast left a hundred and fifty to go, but the road was empty, the weather good, and I went fast, glad to be on the loose at last in Russia, on a straight though not too wide highway between lush pine woods. The responsive wheel took in space that seemed for me alone.

I imagined a Tsar of All the Russias, keen on motoring and out for a spin in his latest car. He had forbidden every other vehicle from the road, and an army corps lined his route from end to end, though sooner or later a band of Nihilists would elude the cordons and lob bombs which would kill him. Or, realising the danger, the tsar would have a well-lit tunnel built from St Petersburg to Moscow, and enjoy his practice runs in that until, again, the inevitable explosion shattered his windscreen.

A man stood by the roadside, cap on, haversack over one shoulder, and fishing rod at the trail. Offering him a lift, I saw he was about sixty and pale faced, with a broad forehead narrowing towards the chin, and wore black hornrimmed glasses. His teeth were obviously false, and he took off the cap to scratch his bald head, brow deeply lined, thin lips breaking into a smile of greeting. I asked where he was going.

'Along the road!' He pointed onwards, ever onwards, so I told him to stow his tackle in the back, and opened the door. He banged my shoulder, at such good luck on hearing my destination was Leningrad. When I added that I would be going on to Moscow, Kiev and Chernovtsy his eyes sparkled with admiration and envy, as if he had dreamed of such a journey and would have given both arms to go with me. But I was wrong. He had been to all three places and many others, had done more travelling that I had, proved when he stabbed his chest: 'Berlin! Soldier!' which made me glad to be giving him a lift.

We didn't speak for a while. Having another person in the car, I tended to look more back than forward in my life, which I didn't much like, so I concentrated on the way ahead. There was a language difficulty of course, certain key words being absent from my vocabulary, while it was perilous to use hand signals at the wheel. I gathered that his name was Vanya, and he had been fishing on the Gulf of Finland, but hadn't caught anything as far as I could see, though he may have sold his catch in Viborg. He talked as if I understood every word, and I drew on my intuition, using a few words and bits of rudimentary grammar, but mostly with little success. I regretted not studying more in London.

Speeding along pleasantly enough, he remarked that the car was a very good 'machine', and wanted to know – I assumed – where it was made, the horsepower, how much the fuel tanks held, what its consumption was at top speed, its age, and the price paid for it. Liking his company and amiable curiosity I explained as much as possible. I'd have liked to know about him, and cursed Nimrod's Tower of Babel for making things so difficult.

More than halfway to Leningrad, we came to the Gulf of Finland, the island fortress of Kronstadt visible in the distance. Beyond the 1939 frontier at Belo Ostrov more cars and buses were on the road. Seeing people strolling along the sidewalks near the beach I realised it was Sunday. Villas, datchas, hotels, cafés and filling stations were frequent at Sestroretsk, the chief place of the resort coast and open-air lounge of Leningraders. Big houses from the old days that had belonged to the upper classes of St Petersburg had been turned into rest homes.

I stopped at a modern cafeteria providing bowls of rich borscht with meat and sour cream, bread, cakes and bottles of cherryade. Women at the next table in plain frocks and kerchiefs were tackling an enormous meal. Most diners were young men and girls in shirtsleeves and summer dresses, and I thought how interesting it would be to speak to them, but I was content enough to observe. Should I try to make contact they would no doubt have looked puzzled and turned away. Never an easy or habitual part of a group, I preferred to be anonymous, to look and listen, like a fish in water, storing up images and memories for the future.

Vanya tried to pay for our meals, but I had enough Russian to indicate that since he was a passenger in my car he had the status of a guest, and I was the one to fork out.

Repino was named after Repin the landscape painter, who lived in the village till his death in 1930. We raced by the place near which Pushkin had fought his fatal duel. When the road broadened into a motorway – light standards, bridges, blocks of flats to either side – Vanya confirmed that he wanted to be let

off in the middle of Leningrad. Traffic signals were too high to
see at times, so I sharpened my sight and slowed down. I must
have drifted into the wrong lane, and funnelled left instead of
going straight on. Being lefthanded, it was another unintended
fork taken that day. A treacherous instinct led me to assume I
was still on the right track for the centre of town, expecting to be
at the Astoria Hotel in fifteen minutes.

Vanya tapped me on the shoulder: '*Abratna!*'

I smiled, not knowing what the word meant.

'*Abratna!*' he repeated.

A beautiful word, which I thought might signify handsome or
pretty. He tapped his forehead, as if to show I'd gone crazy, and
that he would soon be in that state if I didn't take in what he was
trying to say. He resigned himself at my ingrown dimness, till
calling again: '*Abratna! Abratna!*'

Assuming the word to mean other than it did exposed a vital
fault in my restricted vocabulary. He used it so often in the next
ten minutes that I was sure I'd remember it for the rest of my
days. What was he trying to say? '*Abratna!*' – bollocks to
abratna. Never heard such a word. How should I know what it
meant? But he was trying to tell me, in all kinds of ways and the
waving of hands. I couldn't see him face on, though didn't
suppose it would have made much difference. He shrugged,
and pointed to the heavens, for which I didn't blame him when
I looked up the word later. He thought I was either off my head,
or realised only too well what he meant and, in my barmy
foreign way, didn't care. He tried every method of semaphore to
make me understand, while I endeavoured to read what was in
his mind. I knew Russian for turning left or right, but the verb
'to go back' (*abratna*) I hadn't yet come across, possibly because
in my ever-feckless way I hadn't foreseen the use of it.

Blocks of city flats gave place to flimsy cottages in acres of uncultivated flatness. By turning left so soon I had lost the main road into the city, and was heading out of the conurbation. Vanya was in glum despair at my not understanding, assuming in his cloud of pessimism that I may even plough on as far as Murmansk, him unable to stop the car without killing us.

He came back to life when the long moving penny finally dropped and I backed into a potholed side lane to turn around. '*Abratna!*' he cheered.

'*Abratna!*' I cried as he gave me a clap on the shoulder that almost sent me to the middle of the road. We smoked nearly half a packet of Pall Mall before drawing up outside the hotel at half past four. By now the best of friends, and in full view of the gilded onion domes of St Isaac's Cathedral, he wrote his full name on the page of a small pad, and his address which was only a few minutes away on Gorki Street, saying as we shook hands that I must call on him some time, when we could eat, drink and indulge in endless toasts of good vodka.

I went into the hotel to see about my room, not unhappy at being out of the car for a couple of days. I had driven on the left in England, changed to the right in Denmark, gone back to the left in Sweden, and switched once more to the right in Finland, so what were a few *abratnas* to me? It was no wonder that I had ended up speeding to Leningrad mostly down the middle of the road, and strayed off it twice.

I unpacked, and showered, the rush of cold water a blessing, then changed and went to the lobby where I was greeted by a hefty young man wearing black-framed spectacles. He spoke good English, and told me his name was George Andjaparidze who had been seconded by the Writers' Union as guide, factotum and companion during my stay in the Soviet Union.

His duty, he said, in a humorous and immediately likeable tone, was to make sure I didn't get into any difficulties, or trouble with the traffic police, while on my travels. It was a gesture of the Writers' Union's solidarity and concern, he went on. They wanted me to be well looked after, because a foreign writer who could not speak the language was bound to need help in navigating strange and complicated cities.

I supposed he was right, and was happy to meet him, though didn't want to say that I felt more than capable of finding my way to Rumania on my own. But I did hint as much, and he said he didn't doubt my abilities as a motorist, but all the same he was very experienced at getting about, for he had travelled a great deal by car in Russia with his uncle, camping along the highways to and from holidays in the Crimea and the Caucasus.

He had studied at Moscow University and written a thesis on Oscar Wilde, and was now working on a postgraduate dissertation on the books of Evelyn Waugh. 'So we'll have plenty to talk about, and learn from each other,' he said with a broad wink to indicate that we were bound to enjoy the trip.

I showed him the car outside, which he immediately called Peter Peugeot, in honour, he said, of the greater Peter who had founded the city. He arranged for it to be stabled in a special compound nearby, where it would be guarded by an old soldier for a rouble a day. I would not, therefore, need to take the wing mirrors and windscreen wipers up to my room.

I had always liked the sound of 'Leningrad', a solid word, as if with such a name the city could never have been anything but immovably fixed to the centre of the earth – in spite of being built on a swamp. Spread over a vast plain, domes and broad avenues shone in white-night sunlight, the geometrical and artistic layout suggesting that Leningrad was still the capital of Russia.

In the war it suffered more than any other Russian city from the plague of German Nazism, when a million inhabitants had starved to death or been killed by bombardments and air raids. But the place had survived, and communism had continued to dominate people's lives, though not perhaps for most of them their hopes. Living under such discipline they managed from day to day, as is always the case, supporting the barely endurable weight of their rulers, though I didn't see anyone without bread or shoes or a place however small to sleep in. Over much of the Third World the Soviet Union supported insurgencies, while the intelligent Russian realised that the high cost could only come off their backs.

In the park the atmosphere was relaxed, in the warm softness of evening. A young man played a Beatles tape: 'We all live in a yellow submarine . . .' and two Swedish mariners were trying to kiss a couple of Russian girls.

I went with George to a Caucasian restaurant on the Nevsky Prospekt, and ate the best and largest meal since leaving London. He certainly knew the places to go, which was so much in his favour that my dream of motoring alone quickly faded. After sharing a bottle of vodka and a few fragrant wines from the land of his ancestors, I chaffed him at having taken on the onerous appointment of looking after someone like me.

'My dear fellow, it will be a pleasure. They were queueing up by scores to get the job, and I was delighted when it was given to me,' spoken in such a tone as to imply that if I believed that I would believe anything.

In our semi-inebriated condition we strolled along the Nevsky Prospekt hoping to wear off some of the food and drink. At twenty-four he was a man of the world, sophisticated, intelligent, charming and well informed, as well as being entirely open with me. He had already been married and divorced, and had a child, he told me with a pronounced wink under a street lamp, a girl he sees as often as possible, for he was still on good terms with the mother. He now had a wonderful girlfriend, who was most upset by his absence from Moscow.

I looked out of my window at the Hotel Astoria, at the dome of St Isaac's, red sky spreading left and right to cover the whole panorama. People walked the streets at a quarter to one, and buses still slid around the cathedral in the huge square. Living for the moment more easily than I could, youngsters clutched their tape recorders and transistors. The radio behind me gave no interesting news. Going by the squall of deafening static some stations seemed to be jammed by Russian censors, endeavouring to cut out the wail of pop music perhaps, or the drone of information.

Monday, 11 June

Thirteen hundred roubles had been put into my Russian bank account by two magazine publishers, as payment for extracts from *The Loneliness of the Long Distance Runner* and *Road to Volgograd*. I collected the newly minted notes as if they were alms for a pilgrim that would see me through the country and yet, having come so easy and unsolicited, they seemed hardly real.

'Money only ever did when I had to run urgently and buy food, or put it by for the rent man, which I haven't had to do for nearly ten years,' I said to George, who helped me with the formalities.

Stuffing the Monopoly notes into my wallet I complained that any left over at the end of my stay couldn't be taken out and changed into other currencies. He replied that I should just enjoy spending what a Russian labourer had to keep his family on for a few months. I'd never had the equivalent of nearly four hundred pounds in my pocket at any one time, so could feel rich.

On my previous visit to Leningrad, four years before, I'd met Maria Abramovna Shereshevskaya of the university, who had survived the siege as a child and now had a sixteen-year-old daughter. With her friend Galya she had done some of my stories into Russian, and they were now translating the works of Joyce Cary. I was taken with them to Tsarskoye Selo – renamed Pushkin. It was gratifying to reflect that the poet had at last got his own back on the tsar, as poets invariably do on those who torment them, even if only posthumously. To the north of the Great Palace there was a bronze figure of Pushkin on a garden seat by the sculptor R Bach.

Sitting with tea and cakes at a café we talked about the relationship between Russia and England, of how they flirted with each other in the sixteenth century, when Ivan the Terrible made an offer for the hand of Queen Elizabeth I, stating that she 'would be kin to his friends, but hostile to his enemies, and he would be the same to hers'. Good Queen Bess thanked him for his goodwill, but suggested he marry Lady Mary Hastings, about whom the Tsar's envoy reported back that she was 'thirty years old, tall, well built, has a clear complexion, grey eyes, red hair, a straight nose, and long fingers'.

Mary thought it might not be a bad match, since men were becoming scarce for women of her age, but then she heard of his 'barbarous manners' and turned him down, even though he promised important concessions to an English trading company.

Ivan was a man of unlimited self-indulgence and a ferocious

disposition. During his six-week occupation of Novgorod he had 60,000 of its inhabitants slain and thrown into the river. The city of Tver, with a history of incessant devastations, lost 90,000 of its people due to his cruelty. He was to beat his son to death in a prolonged fit of rage, dying from grief and remorse soon after.

Tuesday, 20 June
My first trip on a hydrofoil took us along the coast to Petrodvorets, a smooth ride, and comfortable except for a queasily strong smell of high octane fuel. The out-of-bounds naval base of Kronstadt was half concealed by the haze of Leningrad, a picture that might have been done by Turner.

The half-full hydrofoil eased its way to the landing stage, and we walked into the park along a canalised stream called the Ropcha. After great aquatic leaps from the terrace of the palace its water fed numerous fountains to either side before flowing into the sea.

In front of the palace, where the waterfall filled a pond, was a bronze-gilt figure of Samson parting a young lion's jaws from its tonsils, the ferocious combat frozen in an everlasting pose. Samson knew what he was trying to do, while the noble lion wondered at such vicious purpose, when all it had done was thoughtlessly stray into a vineyard and roar at someone disturbing its enjoyment of the grapes.

The lion could never be as savage as Samson, who endeavoured with maniacal strength to break his adversary unto death. The sculptor Kozlovski had well caught the pitifully tragic scene of the contest, in which God had ordained that Samson do something previously unthought of by man or animal, who both realised when it was far too late that they had been coerced into a situation that could only have one end. From the anguished lion's mouth a jet of water spurted sixty-five feet high, as thick as a man's arms, liquid which might as well have been blood.

The Great Palace, with a façade nine hundred feet long, had been gutted by the Germans, not as an act of war but out of gleeful Teutonic spite. Only the exterior had been restored, to give some idea of what it had once been. The Marly House in the park had been built as a country mansion for Peter the Great so that he could contemplate his new fleet on manoeuvres in the Gulf. Its exquisite proportions were reflected in the surface of a rectangular sheet of water. I viewed the house from a distant point, the one sight from the complex of parks and palaces I would want to remember. I was told that fish in the lake were, until recently, summoned for feeding by the ringing of a certain tone of bell. Rye flour was given to them in accordance with Peter's wishes; he had stocked the water with carp and chut from Prussia.

An oak tree began life as an acorn taken from George Washington's garden. Planted on the Tsarina's Island, it had been presented to Nicholas I in 1838 by the supercargo of an American ship calling at St Petersburg. I pencilled the ways of our several miles' walk on a plan in the *Blue Guide* so as not to forget the marvels no sooner were they behind me. Maria Abramovna had booked a car for one o'clock, to take us back to the hotel.

In the afternoon George and I perambulated the Petersburgian quarters associated with events in Dostoevsky's novels.

Wednesday, 21 June

A pink mist illuminated the cupolas and façades of buildings around the hotel, streets already busy as I collected the car from the parking compound, giving the guard a few extra roubles for keeping it safe. We were going to Moscow.

Luggage was stowed, and Maria Abramovna, who would go as far as Novgorod and return to Leningrad by bus, brought flasks of tea, coffee and sandwiches for the road. She then guided us out of the city by the Ismailovsky and Moskovsky Prospekts.

Traffic was heavy in the suburbs, mostly lorries and buses, but there was less after the right fork indicating Estonia and Kiev, and I took the road straight on for Moscow.

Clouds were low, the land flat and livid green from a recent saturation of rain. None of us seemed properly awake, and I needed full alertness in overtaking the heavily laden and often swaying two-unit lorries.

George and Maria were my invited guests who had to be looked after, so I tried to keep up the talk and not seem grumpy. Their lives were in my care, and I hadn't driven for a couple of days. Whenever at the wheel in the early morning (and we had left at seven) it was not unusual for me to have, or imagine I might have, a near miss or potential accident. It could be in avoiding someone coming too carelessly out of a side turning, or on making a dodgy attempt to overtake, but today all went well because the road was straight and fairly empty. I kept the speed at fifty for a while, then let it creep up to sixty as my senses sharpened. There was no cause to worry, in any case, because it didn't matter what time George and I got to Moscow. My speed went up to seventy.

In Western Europe one could find somewhere to stay the

night with no trouble, but hotels in Russia had to be pre-booked and a schedule maintained. Moscow was almost five hundred miles away, and I'd been advised in Leningrad to cover the distance in two stages, but having set off early I hoped it could be done in one without mishap – or disaster.

We had breakfast by the roadside, and did the first 200 kilometres to Novgorod by ten o'clock. I parked by the bus station so that Maria could buy her ticket back. Novgorod the Great was now a quiet and pleasant town, with wooden houses on the outskirts, and blocks of flats and public buildings in the middle. Trees, gardens and wide streets increased the feeling of somnolent relaxation, very much in line with how we felt.

Near the Kremlin I decoded the word *kvass* on the side of a barrel-shaped wagon where people were standing with jugs and bottles. Being thirsty, and not so far having tasted the beverage, I joined the throng and asked the woman to give me some. For a few kopecks she drew half a litre from the spigot of a light brown liquid which went smoothly down my dry throat and benefited the stomach as well. Maria said it was made from fermented rye bread and flavoured with raisins, and she also enjoyed a mug, though George disdained it. I felt refreshed, and was glad to know you could get it on street corners almost any time of the day.

Some of the churches and monasteries within the walled and fortified Kremlin had been blown up or damaged by the Germans, precious frescos by Novgorod painters lost for ever. I hoped no other calamities would ever befall the town.

A wooden stairway up the side of a tower led to the walls, giving a south and easterly vista of flat fields and sluggish rivers. Slender spires and coppery domes above white churches seemed to doze on the silver green landscape.

Sitting over glasses of lemon tea, in a circular café of many windows outside the Kremlin, an old woman paused in her sweeping between the tables and asked Maria Abramovna if I was an Estonian. If so perhaps you would allow me to talk to him. I regretted not being from that country, for she might have had an interesting story, but on being told I was English she went away sadly, shaking her head.

After two hours in Novgorod George and I had to get on, so walked Maria to the bus stop and said goodbye, promising to send each other books. She wanted a copy of *The Rats and Other Poems*, as well as *A Tree on Fire* when it came out in a few months – both sent with pleasure.

Just after midday we crossed the Volkhov, and I asked George if we couldn't stop in a village and buy a wagon of *kvass*, tow it behind the car and slake our thirsts from it now and again in the warm and sunny weather.

'The roubles may be burning your pocket,' he said, 'but it's an impractical idea,' so instead we savoured large Havana cigars bought on the Nevsky Prospekt, and he likened us to a couple of swollen plutocrats out for a spin.

Cruising at sixty, a car overtook us at more than seventy. Others went by at the same rate, showing D-letters for Germany on their rear ends. 'Did you notice them?' I said. 'Blazoned along the sides was "Berlin–Moscow Rally – 1967".'

Though I had seen no such thing he half believed me. 'I'm feeling too lazy to overtake,' I said.

'You'd be crazy to try.'

'I suppose so,' I went on. 'There's no hurry as far as I'm concerned. If I've learned anything at all in my life it's never to compete. We still have 500 kilometres to do before getting to the greatest kremlin of them all, so we can take it easy.'

More cars of the same breed jet-engined by, serious drivers in shirtsleeves and eye shades, and navigating companions with binocular straps around their necks intent on outspread maps. For some reason George became agitated: 'Do we overtake, or not?'

'I will if you want me to. Your wishes are sacrosanct as the Russian guest in this French car with an English driver.'

Putting the speed up to seventy, perhaps a little more, brought us to the tail of the German column. 'My father was in the Red Army,' he said, 'and was killed in action on the way to Berlin with his brothers-in-arms.'

I ignored the reference to Evelyn Waugh. 'I'm sorry to hear it, but it took place more than twenty years ago.'

'I never knew him. He came from Tiflis. My mother and aunt brought me up.' Unable to look on him directly, I nevertheless sensed his peculiar froglike twist of the lips. 'They spoiled me, of course – rotten, as you say – though I never complain, because they still do.'

'So the Germans are advancing on Moscow again,' I said, 'instead of retreating back to Berlin with swastikas between their legs. Maybe they'll stop at Kalinin or Klin for schnapps.' I pressed the acceleration a little more firmly, till eighty showed on the dial. Flipping on the blinkers and giving two honks I swung out and hurried along on the other side of the road at ninety, my plain Estate sliding by their chequerboard doors. George's tongue went out, two fingers up.

He was still laughing when we halted to finish off Maria Abramovna's sandwiches, but stopped when the German cars overtook us. Further down the road some drivers had pulled in to do physical exercises, bobbing up and down or throwing beach balls to one another. I flashed by, sounding the horn, which they took as a greeting and waved companionably back.

We gave a lift to a village postmistress because of her heavy bag, and when she got to where she was going we took a woman and her child on board. Setting them down a few miles on, the German column swung by, their blips in the wing mirror, the last one narrowly missing a lorry coming the other way.

Long shallow dips in the road made sufficient dead ground, in which cars from the opposite direction would be completely hidden, a perilous landscape to drive through. Signs warned not to overtake at such places, though not always, and I had to watch out for them. George, on the normal side for a Russian driver, and careful with his signals to get by, must have saved our lives a few times.

By two o'clock we were in the Valdai Hills, though they were so low you wouldn't know it, and in two more hours we turned from the bypass into Torzhok, where Pushkin stayed to enjoy the famous Pozharskiye Ketlety or chicken cutlets, named after the owner of the hotel.

In 1147 the town was devastated by the Prince of Suzdal, and between 1178 and 1215 it suffered fire and rapine four times at the hands of rival princes. Then the Tartars slaughtered all the inhabitants on their way to deliver a similar blow to Novgorod. In 1245 and 1248 the Lithuanians did their butchery, and during the wars between the sons of Alexander Nevski more catastrophe was meted out. It was again destroyed by the Tartars in 1327, then the Grand Duke of Moscow occupied and ravaged it. In 1372 the Prince of Tver levelled the place. It grew again, in hope and vigour, but nothing availed, and the town was forcibly annexed to Moscow in 1477, which gave it no protection, for in 1609 it endured its greatest blow when the pillaging Poles burned monks and others alive in their churches and monasteries. It then settled down for 300 years, until the Germans laid it waste in 1941.

While tanking up with petrol beyond that ill-fated place the Germans passed us again. I was no longer interested, and neither was George. In ten minutes we got by them nevertheless. It was difficult not to. I changed gear, charged along with the needle rising, till most of the column was behind. With full steam up, and careful to avoid lorries lumbering from the other way, I got by the final car. I had just finished telling George I couldn't remember what, when, once again, they weren't far off.

The cat-and-mouse game broke up the ennui at being on the road. They fell behind, no sign of them. Bypassing Kalinin, and crossing the long bridge over the Volga at five in the afternoon, my eyes ached from hunger. Maria's goodies had long since gone, so I asked George if he knew of a restaurant along the road. He didn't: 'Don't worry about eating. Just hang on for another hour or so and you'll be at your hotel, where you'll be able to have a very splendid meal indeed.'

'It's all right for you. It's hard work being the driver. When I get hungry I must eat, otherwise I'm liable to make mistakes. I wouldn't like you to be delivered to your mother and aunt's place grimacing from the misted up inside of a plastic bag. Nor would I like to be sent back to London in the same style. The Writers' Union wouldn't like that, for either of us.'

Before my screed convinced him he tried one more throw. 'Places along the road aren't good enough for someone like you, who comes from the capitalist West.'

While he was figuring out the meaning of an expletive which had something to do with the size of the cigar he was smoking,

I stopped in the next village on seeing the word *stolovaya* over the door of a red-bricked building. A gate in the neat blue fence led through a flower garden to the door of the canteen. We stalked in and sat at a table, George looking like a younger version of the man on a Michelin map cover stranded in a place that wasn't worth a star.

A stout woman in a white overall at the serving hatch called out that no meals were available, which seemed good news to George, but on seeing my disappointment, and my raddled features after so long at the car, she laughed and, in a few minutes, produced bowls of scalding soup, then ham, a few slices of black bread, butter, cakes, and again the same old bottles of prune juice, all of it delicious to a starving man. Even fastidious George sampled some, till we both felt fit enough for the last hundred miles to Moscow.

Our German friends were by now far in front, and there seemed little hope of coming first in the unacknowledged race. We couldn't care less, of course, while puffing on our superb cigars. Not talking for a while, a few historical dates knocking about in my otherwise empty head, I recalled having left London on the 12th, and reckoned that today must be the 21st. History, one of my many interests, told me that on 22 June 1941, in the early hours of the morning . . .

'George, do you know what date it is?'

'I never ask myself such a thing.'

'Well, do it now. What's the bloody date?'

'How should I know? I was told on what date to meet you in Leningrad, and I did. Now I'm in your hands. Why should I show any interest in the calender?'

'It's the 21st of June, and tomorrow will be the 22nd. Don't you know what happened in 1941?'

He looked sideways at me. 'Of course I do. The Great Patriotic War began.'

'In which your father died.'

'Correct. And so?'

'Tonight is "on the eve", if you catch my meaning. Twenty-six years ago the March on Moscow began. Perhaps that column of smart little cars is going there, to celebrate in the morning. They're full of middle-aged men, and the timing can't be accidental. After Moscow they'll push on to Kharkov and Kiev, swapping yarns, standing on hills with their old staff maps, and with binoculars around their necks wondering when there'll be a next time and talking about how was the first time.'

Usually quick and intelligent, and smart on the uptake, he said nothing for half a minute, though much must have been fluttering through his mind. It was six o'clock, and the day was far from dark, patches of forest to either side of the road, a glittering lake like a large stamped-out coin fresh from the mint, isolated dwelling blocks and a workshop here and there.

'Catch them up,' he said quietly.

'Beat them to Moscow? They've got too much of a start in their fast little cars.'

'Yours is faster. You're a good driver. When I was told to meet you in Leningrad and stay with you as far as Rumania I added up the distance in my uncle's atlas. It came to 2,500 kilometres, so I naturally feared for my safety at being in the car with an English writer who would keep stopping to drink whisky from a bottle under the dashboard. Luckily you aren't like that. You have so many maps to carry there's no space for bottles.'

'Whoever taught you English certainly did a good job, but I don't need flattery. Did you learn it from the BBC?'

He thought I'd given up the chase, saying glumly: 'We have good professors of languages in the Soviet Union.'

I stepped up the speed. 'It won't be easy, unless they've stopped for another session of physical jerks. But we'll mount a surprise counterstroke and see what can be done.'

I went like a sword of light along a sheet of chromed metal, though careful to stay alive, my heart calm enough as we caught up with them about thirty miles from Moscow. Overtaking a couple, I didn't suppose they were even aware of our game, though the densest should have had some inkling by now.

One, two more – watch that lorry – then another. George slapped my shoulder. 'Nine more to go.'

'Just do me a favour,' I said, 'and light another couple of those choice Havanas. Then we shall see.' With a not unpleasant smell of ordure from such smokes, we devised a formula for getting quickly and safely by as much traffic as possible. To avoid a too-cautious coming out into the empty-enough lane George would lean from his open window.

'Clear?' I'd ask.

'Go! *Davai!*' and out I would shoot, which made for rapid overtaking now that the die was cast.

Or I would call: 'Clear?'

'For God's sake – NO!' and I would hold my place. More of their cars were left behind. We thought the main body of the group might already be in Moscow, but I was enjoying the chase. Speed was exhilarating, but to give myself heart and soul to such a challenge would have blighted my pride

There the rest of them were stalled behind a slow heavily laded Russian lorry, before a long section of roadworks. It was hard to say at first why they weren't overtaking, until I saw a sign demanding single file traffic. Like good socially responsible people they were obeying the law, though the empty road ahead was wide enough for two files. Nor was anything coming the other way.

Here was a time for lateral thinking, which I thought Edward de Bono would approve, or Liddell Hart for a manoeuvre of the 'indirect approach'. 'All clear?'

'*Davai!*' George cried again.

With blinkers doing their job, and sounding V in Morse, I ran along the side of the column till every car was left under the arse of that splendid Soviet lorry. The no overtaking rule persisted for another mile, hard to think why, and they couldn't soon follow because heavy traffic now streamed from the other direction. I smothered my anxiety till getting unscathed – and unseen – back on to the legal side of the road.

'A good thing no highway policeman is on our trail,' George said as we went on like respectable citizens who would never even think of doing anything so wrong – or foolish – as to disobey the regulations.

We passed the motorway ringroad around Moscow at eight o'clock, dusk coming on. I was hungry again. 'A motor car eats up the chauffeur as well as petrol,' I said to George, but now we were within easy range of the hotel. Having left Leningrad that morning, we ran freely along a dual carriageway towards the centre of a twentieth-century metropolis, between white and pink blocks of flats, cranes around some still under construction poking into the empty sky. A television transmitting tower seemed like a needle of Nimrod hoping to draw blood from God with his arrow. We had brought the good news from Aix to Ghent, whatever the news was, though there must have been some. George was happy at being nearer home, and I was glad to have done the trip without an accident, and had a bit of fun on the way. I set him down at his mother's flat, then went on down Gorki Street, turning left to the Hotel Metropole in Sverdlov Square.

Thursday, 22 June

I stood at my hotel window wondering how to spend the day, though I needn't have worried, since my diary showed plenty to do.

The room was on the back and away from street noise, overlooking a courtyard that was small in proportion to surrounding buildings. Clouds above roof slopes were as if trying to decide on the time to let down rain. A slim and pretty girl wearing blue overalls and headscarf straddled the apex of a nearby roof replacing a tile. I stared till she turned and fluttered her fingers at my friendly wave.

I was waiting for the telephone to ring, and hear that George was downstairs. Hundred-rouble notes smouldered in my pocket, and he could help me to spend one or two. The girl clambered to another join of roofs, which I thought a slightly safer position, to chip at excess mortar. I liked watching her skill with hammer and chisel, and how she debonairly (as well as mischievously) sent flakes of plaster skimming downwards. She was happy, I supposed, at having no overseer close enough to watch over her.

I was sorting things for the laundry but looked at her now and again, saw that she had stopped working to gaze across the rooftops as if dreaming of better days. She smiled, and waved, and I beckoned her closer, even into my room, if she liked. Broken clouds framed her, and she seemed to crave a more compatible life on gazing between them. Next time I looked she was adjusting her headscarf before putting in a few more minutes of work. Then as a joke she indicated that I go over the roof to join her. I made to climb out of the window, but the telephone rang and drew me back.

George said he wouldn't be able to show me around the city because of an upset stomach. His mother, a doctor, found him in bed, unusual so late in the morning: 'What's the matter? Why aren't you getting up? You'll be late meeting your English writer.'

'I'm as sick as a dog,' he moaned. 'My stomach's full of razorblades.'

'My poor darling' – she reached for a thermometer – 'it must be something you picked up on your travels yesterday. What restaurants did you eat at?'

'We called at a *stolovaya* for a snack. The Englishman was hungry. He insisted.'

She lifted her hands. 'Oh George, why are you always so careless? How many times have I told you never to eat in those filthy proletarian places?'

I chaffed him. It couldn't have been the food, since I was perfectly well. 'Perhaps you're ill from puffing at too many cigars. Or you're not sick at all, more like, but lolling in bed with your girlfriend. If that's the case I hope you'll feel better soon.'

I walked back to the window, saw rain splashing on to the rooftops. The fair tiler had gone, and taken the packet of American cigarettes I'd left for her on the sill.

Sweeping items off the shelves with my unexpected windfalls of cash, everything seemed so cheap, like being on a looting expedition, George said. He was still pale after yesterday's meal, as I parked the car outside the GUM department store.

He recommended records as bargains, so I bought a box of

ten by Chaliapin, and as many as could be found of Shostakovich, which included the complete *Katerina Izmailovna of Mtsensk*, and *Stenka Razin* with a text by Yevtushenko. My hand went out for the 'Leningrad' Symphony No. 7, and then I picked up a set of Prokofiev's ballet score *Romeo and Juliet*, also a couple of dozen works by Scriabin, Moussorgsky and Tchaikovsky – music from the finest voices and orchestras of the USSR.

We came out of other departments laden with fur hats, balalaikas, Palekh boxes, *matrioshka* dolls, packets of Chinese brick tea, and more Monte Cristo cigars.

In the evening I was taken around the newly opened 'Library of Foreign Literature', millions of volumes from all countries in their original languages. Walking the stacks of so many treasures proudly pointed out, I recalled my first visit to a Nottingham branch library as a child, and a few years later to the main one in the city centre.

The lady in charge led me into a large hall, to give a poetry reading before several hundred people. Out of respect I decided to perform standing, as I nearly always did in any case. But my legs shook so violently that I thought of sitting, though didn't, because the lower part of me was hidden by a curtained table. The affliction must have been due to long walks that afternoon or, more likely, from so many days sitting in the car.

One poem read called 'Love in the Environs of Voronezh' was also the title of a forthcoming book. I wrote the line for its assonance, and because the poet Osip Mandelstam had been exiled to Voronezh during the purges of the 1930s – before being sent off to die in Siberia.

I stood on the pavement afterwards, the Moscow air freshened by a storm of rain. A girl from the audience who introduced herself as Svetlana Filushkina told me she had been born in Voronezh, so I explained why I had used the name, and gave her a copy of the poem so that she would remember why I had done so.

Oksana Krugerskaya and I went by taxi to the Writers' Club, to spend the evening with Frans Taurin. We had met him in Irkutsk four years before, when she had guided me around the Soviet Union.

Relaxed and elated, as one often is from a reading, I was shown to our reserved table in the great dining room. Frans reminded me, after handshakes and the first glass of vodka, of our boozing session by Lake Baikal, when I had walked out on the ice wearing only a thin English mackintosh.

He was a year or so over fifty, but I knew nothing of his life except that he had written novels, and had been on hunting expeditions in the *taiga*. Just above middle height, though not heavily built, he looked physically tough, short fair hair and sharp grey-blue eyes flashing a touch of humour now and again. I could see that he was well able to put on a stance of authority in his new post as a high official in the writers' union, but hoped he did so with sufficient tolerance and generosity.

We toasted absent friends with the first bottle. I spoke little Russian, so Oksana interpreted. What we ate I don't recall, though it must have been good, since the restaurant had a reputation to keep up among those privileged writers who belonged to the Union.

Platitudes and aphorisms flourished as vodka took effect, and for three hours we hardly stopped talking. He seemed to be watching me for signs of collapse, but I foolishly matched him glass for glass, aware of heading for a blackout if such a rate kept up. Hoping to stay conscious till reaching the hotel, a third bottle arrived, and Oksana, who drank only water, became uneasy. Not normally a heavy drinker, I nevertheless assumed that such convivial indulgence was not beyond me, but would I imbibe so much as to make me feel as flat as a board?

The highway to oblivion was in the offing, though the prospect by now seemed not unpleasurable. In London I was used to a few glasses of an evening on needing to relax, so thought I could take my share without losing clarity of speech. My perceptions fought to avoid splitting in two, and did not succeed. One half from its vantage point told me, with hard words and a wagging finger, not to go on too long, while the weaker part scorned its puritanical hypocrisy. I tried to join the two entities, and thereby gain superiority over both, though it was hardly possible, knowing that the fight would only cease in the refuge of sleep. Meanwhile the dam of tight control allowed me at least to continue talking and, in a way, performing.

In the midst of full tables with their shouting parties Frans and I talked about life, art, the duties and freedoms of a writer in a socialist or any other society, issues I was still able to define. All I wanted to do, I said at some point, was get into my car and drive to Siberia – back to Irkutsk – but couldn't because no road went the whole way.

He laughed at my supposing so. 'You're wrong, my English friend. Nowadays there's a wide macadamised highway from Paris to Lake Baikal, and even beyond, take my word for it.'

'But I wouldn't get permission from the authorities to do it, would I?'

'That will come, I'm sure. But you'd have to drive six thousand kilometres before we could do some fishing on the shore at Baikal. Even you would take about a month to do such a journey.'

A good reason for going to Irkutsk again would be to call on Mark Sergeyev, an especial friend from my former visit, a young writer who, with his parents, had been deported from the Ukraine in the 1930s. He told me how, one day after weeks on the railway, his father lifted him up to a slot in the carriage and said: 'Look at all that water. See it? It's Lake Baikal!' I still have the little book he wrote about the region that he came to love.

When I said let's fetch my car from the hotel and set off tonight he stood up stiffly and put out his hand, saying it was time for him to leave. I got to my feet as well, which felt like standing on glass marbles. The gap between me and the rest of the world was so wide it would have needed a long range jet to cross it. People at the next table seemed as if at the wrong end of a pair of binoculars. I supposed that to walk would make me feel more alert. Frans and I shook hands several times in our farewells.

In the urinals downstairs Arbuzov the playwright and the novelist Aksyonov invited me upstairs to their table. Aksyonov, born in 1932, had qualified as a doctor, then wrote *Colleagues*, a novel which became a bestseller all over the Soviet Union. The book was first serialised in *Yunost* (Youth) magazine, edited by the novelist and journalist Boris Polevoi. I had read an English translation, and thought it good, being a brilliant and witty account of three young and idealistic physicians just starting out in life. I was happy to meet him.

Arbuzov offered me a large brandy, which I had the sense to refuse, and they resumed a discussion with several other writers on the art of The Beatles, delighted to have a 'real' Englishman with them and hear his comments, though how serious and knowledgable could I appear with a lake of vodka inside me?

Translated phrases from the long suffering Oksana must have

emerged as pompous clichés, for I told them, though with little conviction, that I didn't much like The Beatles, possibly because my ears couldn't get accustomed to their cacophonies. Writers and intellectuals in England took their work as interesting for reasons I distrusted, but out of good fellowship here in Moscow I added that they were right to find them fascinating and agreeable, since their songs pleased young people all over the world – which they seemed happy to hear. A cynic like me had to guard against the scorn factor, which might be too easily seen as hypocrisy or conceit.

At two o'clock in the taxi queue, still talking, I wondered how long I would be able to hold out, but cars came frequently so I didn't have many minutes to wait. Street lights were dazzling white spheres, and at times I was seeing four instead of two. A lorry shedding clouds of diesel smoke threatened the fragile equilibrium in my stomach. I lit a cigar, as if insanely persuaded that its odour would make me ill, and eventually feel better. I didn't refuse when my friends insisted I take the next taxi.

The doorman at the hotel, practised at spotting a drunk, gave an understanding Russian grin as I handed him a cigar. He saw me into the lift and came up with me in case I stumbled out at the wrong floor, talking sociably all the while, though I took in nothing.

A woman stationed behind a desk at the lift exit came out of her doze to hand over the key, my brain working sufficiently to order – in Russian – a breakfast of caviar and boiled eggs, to be served in my room at nine. She noted it on her pad and went back to sleep.

I walked along the corridor, and found it impossible to get the key in the lock. Must be the wrong one, or someone else's door.

The sky was knocking to come in, and all my life went by, till, I found the right place and my troubles were over. Nothing would be worth worrying about ever again, and I was, with little reason, full of optimism.

It was three o'clock, but life was worth living. A light in the brain scorched my eyes, and I was fixed on a circulating pedestal, like a lighthouse keeper condemned for the rest of his days to a lonely clifftop. I whistled some mindless tune and opened the windows, but the room continued going round like a blinding phosphorescent ocean, candlepower whitening across its turbulence. What day was it? Where was I? Disconnected from upper and nether worlds I wanted to soar over the Himalayas, out of my skin.

I stared at the blank wall, and looked at my watch, as if that could help me. Well, it did: half an hour had gone by. My stomach was burning as if full of liquid lead. Oblivion wouldn't come. It seemed futile to want anything. All I knew was that I had at least kept the flag flying with someone who had hoped to drink me under the table, an observation in no way discouraging as I ran for the bathroom.

Friday, 23 June
Groggy from my late night, yet buoyed by the residue of having been satisfactorily pissed, I called on an editor who asked me to submit an article for his literary magazine, on the writer's relationship to society. Being on holiday – more or less – put me in no mood for such work, and I didn't in any case care to think about problems I couldn't take seriously.

Maybe laziness was my reason for refusal. Essays cost blood, and I had no wish to write what children, students or civil servants penned for the eyes of whoever needed to find out whether or not they were conforming to the conditions of the country they lived in.

Yet I did consider saying yes to that amiable editor, felt almost guilty at turning him down, being flattered that he imagined I had something interesting to write. Articles, after all, give a sense of self-importance not unattractive to a writer of fiction.

Looking through my notebook at some of the material that might have been used, I doubted it would have been suitable, reflections such as:

If religion is no longer permitted to be 'the opium of the people' why should literature be sacrificed for that role? An artist cannot afford to have any religion or political beliefs, because the faith demanded would corrupt and then destroy his liberty, and so his talent.

If a writer has something worth saying it should be put into the mouth of one of his characters, never forgetting to think complicated but write plain. Shun the prevailing culture and only believe in yourself. Whoever thinks – or hopes – that 'the pen is mightier than the sword' becomes society's scapegoat.

In your work don't ask who you are, but help others, if you care to, to know who they are, while careful not to drive them to despair.

A writer must consider himself a shaman who will live for ever. Any feelings of 'class' or hierarchy are too base to be considered. Live through others but don't let them live through you.

So many cracker mottoes perhaps, obfuscations and irre-levancies, and bullshit for a writer who uses imagination instead of a malleable brain. I couldn't have concocted an article that would have been acceptable to the editor of a prestigious Soviet literary journal. But I expressed my idiosyncratic views at a five o'clock poetry reading, and at a party later.

Saturday, 24 June

An Intourist car and driver ferried us to Zagorsk for the day, thus allowing me to give some attention to the landscape. Yet I saw little more than if I had been at the wheel, when one-second glances took in all I thought necessary.

With Oksana, her beautiful daughter Irina, and George, we went forty miles northeast from Moscow, across open rolling land towards the Volga. Descriptions of the Russian countryside I leave to Chekhov and Turgenev, or the paintings of Repin and Levitan.

Zagorsk, with 80,000 inhabitants, was no longer the great religious centre it had been. A walled area in the middle of town enclosed the usual churches and monasteries, palaces and museums. In the fifteenth century the bishops could raise 20,000 men at arms, and in 1608 the place withstood a sixteen-month siege by an army of Poles. Only the Tartars took it, in the Middle Ages, soon after its foundation. Part of Napoleon's army set out from Moscow in 1812 to loot it, but for some reason turned back halfway. It is still a point of pilgrimage, second only to the Lavra at Kiev.

In the cathedral we were caught up in a crush of old and middle-aged women, their string and cloth bags rattling with all-shaped bottles of holy water from the well dug by Sergius the founder in 1342 – which they would take back to their town or village. Most were poor and shabbily dressed in oversized coats, despite the summer day. Some wore men's tightly buttoned jackets, and the face of one woman was so thin I thought she must be close to death. Travel worn and seared by the wind, grey hair showed from under her headscarf. What suffering she must have endured throughout her life! The evidence was overwhelming.

The men among them, with straggling Tolstoyan beards, wore long belted blouses and military style caps, pushing to find a place and continually crossing themselves. Children in Young Pioneer scarves and shirts plastered with communist badges tried to get close to the altar and see the icons. Their young clean faces contrasted with those of the pious and old, and they barged about laughing and shouting to one another, showing no tolerance for the singing of the choir and the priests' solemn incantations. To them it was a museum, and they only wanted to see the unusual objects in it, perhaps also to show off their supposed superiority to the worshippers.

Old people, singing or prostrated, were to them a weird crowd from another world who only made it more difficult to reach the precious objects. One old woman pulled a boy back who pushed too violently by, but he snapped from her grasp and went on into the scrum, calling to boys already lost in it. Her grey eyes glared distress and hatred, wanting to yank him back and give him a good pasting, which George said he and most of them deserved. But she knew it would do no good. The lack of respect was endemic, and a lesson was impossible. The two worlds would never meet. She crossed herself and joined in the singing with a look of ecstasy which made her seem far younger. She would get the most out of being in Zagorsk while she could – or for as long as she lived.

Sunday, 25 June

Driving around the city, with George's navigation. I needed it, because though the layout was more rational than in London there were no proper street maps on sale. The best had no scale, and showed the major public buildings by picture, which confused much of the neighbouring detail.

I had two interviews that day, one with *Pravda* and the other with *Yunost* but I remember little of either, such meetings being always more or less the same. But I also called at Intourist to find out whether the permitted route to Kiev couldn't be altered for a shorter one. I had noticed on the Freytag-Berndt 'Strassenkarte Ost Europa' that the one I wanted branched off just south of Orel, thus avoiding the lengthier drive through Kursk and Poltava.

I was told it would not be possible because the recently built road didn't have sufficient service stations. Another diversion I wanted to make was to the village of Ulashkovtsy – Loshkovitz in Yiddish, Loskowizce in German, and slightly different in Polish and Ukrainian – on the way to Chernovtsy. Before 1918 it had been part of the Austro–Hungarian Empire, but was then allotted to Poland. After the Second World War if fell to the Soviet Union and became part of the Ukraine. In past ages of shifting borders it was overrun by Cossacks, Tartars and Turks, but the Jews survived until the Germans arrived in 1941. The village stands in a sharp elbow of the meandering River Sereth, which flows south into the Dneister.

In 1905 it was a place with an important Jewish community. According to my large-scale Austrian map it was on the eastern bank of the river with, opposite, a synagogue and a *mikvah* – a ritual bathing place. My reason for wanting to call and take photographs was because my mother-in-law had been born there, though it was unlikely she would remember anything: she had left with her family at the age of five for New York and a safer life.

The place was only thirty or so miles off the Intourist route but, to my chagrin, I would not be allowed to go there, though was told that had permission been asked long beforehand it might have been arranged.

In the evening we went to a party at the flat of Valentina Ivasheva, a professor of English literature at Moscow University. She had written textbooks for students on 'British proletarian novelists', and in the chapter dealing with my work said I was the only 'genuine working-class novelist', which seemed no favour to me, who rejected labels of any sort.

A small grey-haired woman, somewhat fierce in her opinions, she was known, George had told me, for generosity to her students, while at the same time having the power to make or break them. He added that she wrote about 'foreign working-class' people because she was afraid of them in her own country, it being in any case more comfortable to write of them than fraternise in real life, a policy I could hardly blame her for, though it amused me all the same.

I sensed she was disappointed that I had so little to say, either about my life, my writing, or my world views. She did ask why I had written *The General*, an anti-pacifist novel set in a war between two totalitarian states. I said I'd simply thought of the plot and used it, adding that the story was a fantasy, while knowing it to be far from the 'proletarian writing' she had foolishly expected.

I was more at ease with her husband, whom everyone called Uncle Dima. He had little interest in literature except to read and enjoy it. An air ace in the war, he was a Hero of the Soviet

Union, having been shot down a few times and still seriously suffering from his wounds.

Surrounded by adoring students in the small flat, he told a joke, a sparkle of humour in his lake-blue eyes, about two lions in a circus sitting peacefully on their high stools. The assistant lion tamer cracked his whip to make them do some tricks, but they haughtily refused to move. He tried again and again. They eyed him disdainfully, so he complained to the chief lion tamer: 'Those bloody lions won't do a thing I tell them.' The chief lion tamer came to see: 'Of course they won't. The stools are too comfortable. Make them sit on jagged rocks, then they'll jump, and do anything you say.'

Everyone had probably heard it before – I had – but they applauded, which pleased Uncle Dima. A few years later he leapt from the window, unwilling to face a helpless and humiliating old age.

Monday, 26 June

I walked through the lobby from the hotel lift with a set of windscreen wipers, two wing mirrors, and a screwdriver, as if on my way to work. There'd been no guarded parking as in Leningrad, so all accessories and whatever was visible had to be taken upstairs every night.

I felt a bit of a fool putting things back in the cool morning air, rush-hour crowds flowing by on the way to their offices. Loot from my shopping included more Cuban cigars of all kinds from the hotel lobby, which seemed of no interest to the Russian clientele. Each colourful box of Partagas, Romeo and Juliets, Uppmans and Monte Cristos cost only a few roubles, and I stacked the car sufficient to see George and me to Chernovtsy, not forgetting to leave quite a few for England.

There were toys for David I'd scooped up from the *Dyetski Mir* (Children's World), a store as big as Harrod's, but with a more warehouse atmosphere. I'd acquired what maps could be found, as well as an immense atlas of the physical world so big it had to be laid flat in the car. The Russians are renowned for high quality cartography, their multicoloured geological maps beautifully showing the soil and rocks of the earth. Perhaps the infinite patience required by such technical expertise holds back the onset of angst, helping cartographers to survive while making the world interesting for those who need to know what it is made of. Beyond political considerations the maps help surveyors and explorers in their field work.

Sorrow at leaving Moscow would be more than made up for by going south. In goodbyes to friends I'd received requests to send books when back home. Valentina Jaques of *Soviet Literature* wanted my volumes of stories, and *A Tree on Fire*. Oksana Krugerskaya asked for that book as well, and pictorial calendars of English scenery.

Tanya Kudraevzeva of *Foreign Literature Magazine* hoped I'd post novels by Laura del Rivo, *Smallcreep's Day* by Peter Currell Brown, the text of *Little Malcolm Against the Eunuchs*, and a couple of my books in French translation. Someone from Intourist requested a copy of *Road to Volgograd* for their library, and I also promised books for Oksana's daughter Irina. These requests were honoured, though I wasn't able to get information on Paul Schofield for the writer Yuri Kovalev.

As I walked back and forth along the hotel front waiting for George, passers-by stopped to look at a small MG touring car parked near mine. It was white, neat and low slung, and many admired something not made in Russia, as I heard said. They examined the dashboard, and would have liked a look at the engine, while the more knowing translated the number plate and the MG insignia, announcing to the others that it was a beautiful British 'machine'.

My more ordinary vehicle drew little attention, its nearest equivalent being the Volga stationwagon, which looked even more dependably robust, but I had no way of knowing how they really compared. At least people were fascinated by the compass fixed to the windscreen, while I stood among them as if the car belonged to somebody else.

Luckily it was pristinely clean, because the previous day I'd had the first fifteen hundred miles of grit and dried mud taken off at a service station, for the cost of one rouble. I'd manoeuvred it up the ramp of the washing machine, doors and windows tightly shut, to be sloshed and thoroughly buffed up, blue liquid pouring down the windscreen. Peter Peugeot shook with hesitation on advancing slowly along the unfamiliar tracks. I wondered if it would stand up to the ordeal, not having the hardiness of Russian vehicles, but the car at last reached level ground, water still swirling and none the worse for the experience.

George arrived bearing flasks of drinks, and large paper bags of food, saying that his mother and aunt had been up most of the night preparing them as supplies for our journey, as if we were leaving for places where nourishment would be unobtainable or, I thought, so that he wouldn't be tempted to eat the 'filthy' food of some roadside *stolovaya*.

His girlfriend stood a few yards off, to bid him farewell. 'As far as Chernovtsy!' she cried. 'You'll never come back, I know you won't!'

At another burst of tears gallant George tried to console her. 'Of course I shall. All I have to do is take the train. My seat's already booked. I'll be back in ten days, my love.'

'The train will crash,' she wailed. 'Don't go. I dreamed last night that you were killed.' She was in his arms, head on his shoulder, shirt and blouse wet from her weeping. 'Please don't go, George, I implore you.'

She was sliding to her knees for more desperate pleading, but he drew her up. 'I must go,' he said, with such a loving and tender kiss that I envied him. He may have been disappointed had she not put on such a performance, but it was plain from her despairing features that she was in exquisite misery at the prospect of his departure. He consoled her as best he could, but finally eased her away at seeing my impatience, though I did try to hide it.

On our way out of town we were stopped by a militiaman for having strayed into a left lane instead of going straight on at a traffic light. Though his whistle blew loud and clear I was for charging on. 'We have to stop,' George said, 'but let me talk.'

I didn't see why we should be pulled up for such a petty fault, or something which seemed no fault at all, but George said that policemen in Russia were very strict with drivers, which was why there were so few accidents.

He explained, with much tact, that I was a foreigner, an English writer unfamiliar with the traffic regulations and the complicated layout of Moscow. His half truths were accepted, but he was told that I ought nevertheless to watch out and stay in the right lane. 'And by the way,' he added, when all I wanted to do was scoot off, 'what kind of car is that?'

George obliged him with as many details as he had picked up along the way. The policeman then asked, pointing at me: 'What kind of books does he write?'

'Proletarian novels,' George said, as traffic flew by in all directions, drivers with smug expressions giving us a wide berth and glad we'd copped it instead of them.

'I'm pleased to have met an English writer, but tell him to stay in the right lane.'

I cursed all the way to the ring road, George horrified at such a bolshie condemnation of the police. 'They're people's police, after all,' he said.

'Of course they are. They're the people's police in every country. They're not fucking Daleks. He might have sounded a bit cultured but he's still a copper, though maybe he wasn't one at all. The Writers' Union hired him from an actors' school and told him to stand there and stop us so that he could say what a fine writer I was and make me feel more at home. On second thoughts perhaps Intourist set it up.'

He forgave my rant, since we seemed to share the same brand of humour. The longer he was with me the more I realised how sophisticated, tolerant and diplomatic he could be, a courtier from having been brought up by two women. Perhaps it was also due to his Georgian ancestry which, so the joke had it, allowed every man to call himself a prince.

Open spaces calmed me. They always did, but the road narrowed, and I was faced with the usual perilous task of overtaking lorries whose rear ends tended to sway across the empty side of the road when I got too close. Those coming from the opposite direction called for equal care.

Serpukhov was bypassed to the east by a new bridge over the River Oka, which I would mark on the map in my room later. George said he had often strolled along the beautiful banks with his girlfriend – not the one he had just said goodbye to – in summertime. A glance showed its water running blue under sunlight between sleaving greenery left and right, with flashes of white sand here and there, a Russian paradise. I felt how pleasant it would be to rent a room in a village for a month and enjoy the languorous days.

'You must come back and do it some time,' George said. 'The Writers' Union would make it possible, since you're their blue-eyed boy. You'd find a nice Russian girl who, believe me, are the best in the world. Then I suppose you'd be happy, at least for a time.'

Best to go on living with my own inner storm, I thought, the powerhouse of a writer. To present it with good treatment would turn it into a war of spiritual attrition. So I would leave the dazzling serpentine Oka alone and concentrate on the road, or go back to twitting George. 'Your girlfriend was certainly upset at you leaving. She was as devoted as Melanya in *A Nest of Gentlefolk.*'

'"Not with all the strength of her soul" though' – he finished the quotation – 'because my girlfriend was angry as well.'

'All the same, it was very touching. I was almost crying myself. Do young women always play up like that when their boyfriends go away?'

'Mine do. Not that it's rare, because women in Russia never know whether or not their men will be coming back. Perhaps it has something to do with the war. They used to say that the way to war was a wide highway, but the way back is only a footpath.'

I was half intoxicated at speeding over such endless tracts of land, so vast we seemed to be going slower than we were, making the scenery somewhat dull. The sun came partially out again, like white wine suffusing the sky. Lorries moving south were laden with iron ore, sand, bricks or crates, so many on the move maybe the railways were overloaded, and though electrified had too few lines to serve the needs of so much industry. Many, however, turned off to places not served by the railway, their space in the column replaced by more vehicles filtering on to the main road north and south. Some were abandoned wrecks just off the verges, and I hoped not because of accidents, though supposed that most were.

Overtaking when it was clear, we made headway, and the impulse of a pleasurable month on the tranquil Oka was ploughed under the wheels of the stalwart Peugeot. We reached Tula three hours after leaving Moscow, trundling over cobblestones and tramlines. Signposts were scarce, or not prominent enough for me to see them without George's help. On my own I would have been at the mercy of my intuition, and got lost, but even he urged me to pull in a couple of times to ask the way. A street plan of the city would have made little difference. I supposed one day there would be a Michelin guide of Russia, with information and town maps to ease the way of bourgeois travellers, yet wasn't sure I wanted one in this hit-or-miss exploring ground.

Twenty kilometres south of Tula I turned right and, after a mile, came to Tolstoy's estate of Yasnaya Polyana, where he lorded it from 1862 until his death in 1910. A gardener told us that the man in charge of the house would be going to lunch in a few minutes, taking the key with him, so we couldn't be shown inside. We were free to enjoy the grounds though.

We wandered among dark and shady elms, pines and oak trees, to Tolstoy's unmarked grave off the path in a small clearing, a hump of earth where he'd wanted to be interred. If I had been wearing a hat I'd have taken it off. No wonder he did so much work, living in the same place for so long. Not that his existence had been peaceful, said George.

A tall elderly, elegant and refined looking old man, in a

stylish brown suit with a watch chain across his waistcoat, came out of the house and greeted us. I talked in French, for his was fluent, with no trace as far as I could tell of a Russian accent. He had been one of Tolstoy's secretaries in the last year or two of the great man's life, and was now a curator of the house and museum. Many people came here, he said, writers among them – oh, how many writers! But there was only one Tolstoy, who has long been at rest at this most beautiful spot on earth.

By the grave was a simple wooden bench Tolstoy had often used. We were told that an English writer had been there recently – he shall be nameless – and had sat on it, insisting someone take a photograph. Maybe I would find his initials on one of the nine trees surrounding the spot, if I cared to look, I said to George.

The house had suffered during the war – furniture smashed, books scattered, manuscripts used to light fires. Maybe the more enlightened – if there'd been any – had sent handwritten sheets back to Germany as souvenirs.

Buses were unloading Russian tourists and an eager band of young scholars. Tolstoy opened a school for peasant children in his house – and trampled his own devils on walks around the estate. He went regularly on foot to Tula and also, on several occasions, the 200 kilometres to Moscow. Our amiable guide, who must have been at least eighty, said he must go to lunch, so we got back in the car.

The compass pointed south to Orel, through more country occupied by the Germans, though you would never have known. Electrification of the mainline railway was complete to the Donbas, and many new factories east of the highway – huge, plain and in light colours – stood near complex transformer stations. We passed the right turn for Turgenev's estate at

Spasskoye Litovinovo and, deciding there was no time to call, went on into Mtsensk, which I knew of from Leskov's story, and Shostakovich's opera *Katerina Izmailovna* seen recently at Covent Garden.

A militiaman on duty at every important crossroads kept an eye on passing traffic. Provided with a sentry box, he usually stood outside. For any minor infringement of the rules, George told me, such as passing him at more than twenty-five miles an hour, or overtaking at the junction, or being a shade too close to the middle of the road, or having a dirty windscreen which might cut down visibility, he could fine you on the spot. The minimum was one rouble, and if you got by without getting fined – not always easy – you said you had 'gained a rouble'.

Without his frequent warnings I would probably have shelled out my literary earnings into the greedy palms of the police. To be on the safe side, George went on, it was better to go by at twenty, though not much slower or he might think you were drunk.

I wondered what I had done wrong, therefore, on being motioned by an unmistakable baton to the verge. 'This is getting monotonous.'

George wound down his window. 'It's only the second time in 300 kilometres,' he said, as the law came over in his blue uniform, peaked blue and red cap, and gave a vague salute. He was young, handsome you could have said, with a dark complexion and leathery skin, and piercing brown eyes showing how bored he must be in that dusty little town mouldering under its own history. 'Where are you from?'

'Moscow.'

'And where are you going?'

'To Kursk,' George said. 'We're tourists.'

'Papers.'

He examined the our passports, then handed them back. 'What sort of a car is this?' He looked at it for a while.

'Ask the bastard if we can go,' I said.

George told me not to be such a hooligan. 'May we go now, officer?'

He waved us on with his stick. 'Don't drive too fast.'

We lit Havanas with the roubles saved. I hadn't been over the limit. We'd been stopped because he'd had nothing better to do. George laughed at the notion as I shot through the rest of town, a pretty place, with its cathedral perched on a thousand-foot cliff.

The weather had been dry so far, even sunny, but disagreeable clouds were assembling to the south. On our way over gentle hills we talked about the novels of Evelyn Waugh, William Golding and Iris Murdoch, and the state of literary criticism in England – which I knew nothing about, though I didn't want to disappoint him.

Soon tiring of that we swapped common curses in both our languages, unable to decide whether English or Russian would get first prize for having so many of the most foul, blasphemous and picturesque. I even invented a few, but can't be sure who won. I could only suppose that the exchange of philological unpleasantries encouraged George to say: 'I must tell you that I feel privileged in spending so much time with a real English proletarian writer.'

'Don't insult me, George, though let me tell you that I'm equally happy to be in the company of a university graduate I can enjoy talking to. I don't have any such friends in England.'

'I'm not sure how I'm meant to take that exactly, but you must tell me about the working class in your country. I haven't even met any Russian workers, in my sheltered life, never mind an English one.'

'First of all, the term "proletarian writer",' I said, 'is an oxymoron that only morons would use, as you ought to know by now, being a fully qualified philologist. And "working class" is a bourgeois definition, used by those who only want to keep the workers in their place.'

'But according to what you write you don't like the Establishment in your country.'

'Who would? The Establishment doesn't like me, and goes on trying to throw its weight about.'

'So don't you want to overthrow it? That's what we are told in our Marxist textbooks.'

I laughed. 'The workers in England are very sensible. All they want is to work less and get more money, and who can blame them? I certainly wouldn't want to see them storming Buckingham Palace.'

He mulled on this for a time, then: 'What you say is very pessimistic, but I suppose I should consider myself lucky in getting such views from the horse's mouth.'

'Have you read it?' I was glad to get off the topic. 'It's a wonderful novel of Joyce Cary's.'

'Of course I have. You'll be asking if I've read Dickens next, or Kingsley Amis. I'm not illiterate. But what about the trade unions? They're very active in England.'

'That's because it helps them to get into Parliament, or the House of Lords. Every sensible person wants to be part of the Establishment, but not me, because I'm a writer.'

'I'm disappointed.'

'In life, George, you learn far more from disappointment than success.'

And so we went on, sometimes slagging each other due to our ignorance of each other's country, which talk finally came down – or went up – to respect and friendship. He was an ideal companion.

In Orel (pronounced 'Ariol'), 400 kilometres from Moscow, our energies were declining. The central tram route through the city was being 'reconstructed' on both sides, which called for slower speed and more care. The usual litany of disasters had happened in the history of Orel only, it seemed, more so. After its foundation by Ivan the Terrible it was ruined by the Tartars, taken by the Lithuanians, sacked by the Poles, and calamitously burned to ashes in 1573, 1673, 1679, 1848, and 1858. The Germans occupied it for two years from 1941, and half the town was devastated by the time they were thrown out. It was now a thriving city, with many industries. All this from George, and I said he ought to be congratulated on knowing so much about his country, which was in some ways rather more than I knew about mine. On the other hand towns had been burned down less often.

On the southern outskirts we stopped for a beer, bumping into a parking space by piles of rubble from the roadworks. At Trosna I saw the sign for the direct road to Kiev, which I was not allowed to take, so pressed on into the Province of Kursk, where the land was more open, and fertile under a recent visitation of rain. The road surface turned black and slippery with mud spilled by tractors crossing from one field to another (if you could call such huge expanses fields) the back window so covered that nothing could be seen, which made George even more necessary as an extra pair of eyes.

The earth was as black as all books said it would be, but with occasional patches of livid green. Stopping, with fifty miles to go before the end of our day, we snacked away the final cutlets, pickled plums and cucumbers packed by George's angelic mother and her sister, and shared the remaining cold tea. The verge was so saturated with rich loam I feared the car would sink to its axles if we stayed too long. I recalled thoughtlessly parking by the roadside in central Finland, on gravel so soft it was impossible for the tyres to grip when we wanted to move. Hardly knowing what to do, it seemed we would be stuck for ever, till half a dozen tall young Finns came from a nearby farm and lifted the car bodily back on to tarmac.

Mentioning this to George, we hurried away and, at eight o'clock, just before nightfall, reached Kursk, 375 miles south of Moscow. I went slowly by trams and parked cars looking for the Intourist Hotel, up straight wide Lenin Street to vast Red Square where, according to the sketch plan in Nagel's guidebook, we would find it. There was no sign, so George got out to enquire, and returned with the information that we must have passed it two miles back up Lenin Street – such were the distances in Russian provincial cities.

Our spartan rooms were adequate in which to change and have a shower. The manager arranged to have the mud-splattered car cleaned, and watched over during the night in its parking slot by the hotel entrance. After our snacks and picnics of the day we fed like lords in the little-patronised eating area, washing the meal down with a hundred grammes of vodka each.

To remind ourselves that we still had legs we took our umbrellas and walked along the wide deserted streets. Rain stopped, and the night air softened, though odours from recent downpours were sharp in the nostrils. Blocks of flats shut off the moon, cushioned in its powdery halo when we glimpsed it, and promising more bad weather. A train hooter sounded, from a string of lighted carriages on their way to Moscow beyond the wooden houses. It was part of my exhaustion to wonder what I was doing in Kursk – of all cities – yet I felt glad to be spending the night in a place that wasn't a capital.

The whistling of another train reverberated over the houses, tugging primevally at the stomach. George suddenly asked what I thought of Stalin. Did he want to know so that he could report my opinions back at headquarters? I need hardly care, but decided to answer seriously, yet without committing myself to complete honesty.

'In what way?' I asked.

'Well, we all know that he wasn't a good man.'

'You can say that again, but I've known it for a long time, certainly before 1952. I was familiar with Arthur Koestler, Victor Serge, and George Orwell, as well as *The Conspiracy of Silence* by Alex Weissberg, and a book about what happened to the Poles after the Russians marched in in 1939, not to mention *The Long Walk* an epic of escape from Siberia to India via the Gobi Desert, by Slavomir Rawicz. No doubt there were many other witnesses. I've always been a hungry reader, an addict if you like, because what else does a writer do except read? A lot of people on the so-called Left in England didn't want to know. All the books I read seemed true enough to me. A lot of Russians must have twigged what was going on, because they were living through it themselves.'

'But do you think Stalin was necessary for Russia?'

'I don't know. That's for the Russians to say. Perhaps only somebody so ruthless could have got the country through its industrial revolution, and held things together in the Great Patriotic War. When I worked in a factory at that time we used to say "Joe for King!", but that was because the Red Army was performing so many miracles.'

The noise of trains in the Tuskar valley seemed to come from a sky unable to hold it in, as if an ache too melancholy to be borne. Rain fell with the sound, which became hard to imagine it had been set off by a train. One thought of those endless strings of wagons down the hill, laden with coal and anthracite from the Donetz mines, and people in their straggling villages, with train wheels rumbling through deep and troubled sleep – but I pondered mostly on journeys to the furthest regions of that enormous country.

Still talking around the same subject, we walked along badly paved streets of wooden houses, all in darkness except one with a television set flickering opposite the half-screened window. 'Tell me, George,' I said, 'how come I'm in Kursk, a place I first heard of in my teens?'

His face was hidden by the umbrella. 'Kismet, my dear chap. Fate is a human affliction – or so I must have read somewhere.'

'I suppose that when you get back to Moscow you'll report all I said about Stalin, especially the etceteras.'

'Why do you think that?'

'You're a member of the Komsomol, aren't you?'

'Of course. You have to be, if you want to get on in our society. But you know, people will be curious as to how we got on together.' I didn't mind when he changed the subject: 'North and south of the Kursk salient,' he said, though who didn't know? – 'the Germans attacked with three thousand tanks and two thousand planes, an offensive they couldn't afford to lose, but did. It was the greatest tank battle in history, and if they had been victorious, Kismet would have been the same for both of us. We wouldn't be talking here in Kursk. But the predators were seen off, so we are.'

The shunting of trains was less audible. People in the centre of town came from the huge House of the Soviets after a concert or meeting. Back at the hotel by midnight, my feet seemed weightless. Tired, I supposed. Things would be livelier in Kiev tomorrow evening, George reminded me.

Tuesday, 27 June

We crossed the empty acres of Red Square – not Red for Revolution but because the word in Russian meant beautiful. Many towns therefore had their Red Square. Out by Dzerzhinsky Street, a wide straight and steep highway headed for the undulating steppe country.

The road turned sharply left at Oboyan so that everyone could, I thought, slow down and see a monument to the Soviet soldiers who died in the battles of 1943.

'Do you want to see the actual ground they fought on?' George knew my interests by now. 'There'll be a museum there as well.'

Morning was the time I wanted to put the greatest possible distance under the wheels, a hundred miles before midday usually guaranteeing a reasonable stretch by nightfall. At my desk writing, if I managed a page or two before twelve o'clock, it was an indication that many more would get done before dusk. Likewise on the road, morning was not to be wasted. Released from sleep and never-remembered dreams, I liked to get as far on as feasible. But cafés were so infrequent that when I saw one close to the monument we went in, for a glass of very weak coffee. 'When Trollope was postmaster general,' I said to George, 'he worked at his novels from five to eight o'clock in the morning, and what a vast amount he wrote.'

Outside, a huge framed map showed the main battlefield, which covered hundreds of square kilometres around Oboyan, a place half hidden in mist and drizzle as we went through. I said to George that it was another of those interesting localities I'd come back to and explore properly.

'I don't suppose you'll do so. Life is far too short. I can see that when travelling by car you only want to get on.'

You certainly do. You can stay in one town all your life with one house, one job, and one wife, and life goes in a flash. If you change job town or wife every year it might seem to go more slowly, but it's all the same in the end. Life *is* short. Everyone was born yesterday. Did one emerge from childhood to reach death so quickly? The beginning and the end are real enough, but as soon as you start thinking of the dream in between it's gone already. We talked a lot on that long journey.

Beyond Bielgorod the sky was clearer. We were in the Ukraine, where the black and fertile top soil was said to be seven feet deep. Entering Kharkov, a city of a million people, I needed to find a service station, because the indicators hadn't functioned since leaving Moscow, and even with George's expert assistance it was hazardous overtaking. 'The chances of getting them repaired are slight,' he said on hearing that even the Peugeot agent in Helsinki had failed to do so.

No service station was marked on our rudimentary town plan, but George enquired from several people till we found one. I teased him about the dearth of good maps and clear signposts, which made it so difficult in cities. 'The authorities must be afraid of giving away military secrets. Or isn't the signpost factory fulfilling its five-year plan?'

'Travelling to remote places, you don't say at the end that you found your way there,' he said, 'but that you *talked* your way there. If you don't use your mouth on the road in Russia you don't get anywhere. In any case, don't you know there's a Ukrainian proverb which says "Your tongue will lead you to Kiev"?'

The garage, in a cul-de-sac near the city centre, had its gate locked. George called through the wooden bars to an old woman sitting on a bench outside the office. When she put down her knitting and came over he explained that we were in an important foreign car that needed looking at by an expert mechanic. 'We're in a great hurry to get to Kiev, so please open the gate.'

'The manager won't like it if I do. The workshop is full of cars already, and there's no space in the yard.'

George pointed out that the yard was almost empty.

'I know, but we're expecting twenty cars any minute, and they've been booked for repairs for the last three months.'

'They may well have been,' he went on, 'but the fact is, Comrade Gatekeeper, that this man' – pointing to me – 'is a foreigner whose machine is in a dangerous condition.'

I stood by the car feeling scruffy and dead beat, and no doubt looking it, as is the case as soon as one stops, even though after only four hours at the wheel. Her attractive pale blue eyes were very much alive for her age: 'I can't help that,' she said.

George talked on with quiet intensity, as if conducting a flirtation, suggesting that if he continued in that way he would end by asking her in no uncertain terms to become his fiancée. She blushed, hoping her reputation in the district wouldn't suffer if she gave in. George employed the same tone, and I felt like cheering him on, while not understanding a word. He certainly knew how to deal with motherly Russian (or Ukrainian) ladies, but what did it matter to him?

I already wanted to say that since nothing was fundamentally wrong with the car we should press on and try our luck in Kiev, but he wouldn't hear of it, and pursued his courtship ritual, unwilling, even perhaps unable, to break off.

'I can't let you in under any circumstances,' she said, though with lessening resistance. 'It's more than my job is worth.' And yet, as if hypnotised by his rigmarole, even while talking, she took a key from her apron and slotted it in the lock. 'It's not that there's no room. There's just so much work at the moment, so I can't let you in.' She turned the key. 'You should have informed us in advance. You could have telephoned from Kursk or Voronezh, or wherever you've come from.' With admiring eyes still on him she pulled the gate open so that I could drive in.

The manager came from his office, looked at the car, and suggested that since it was covered in mud I should put it through the washing machine. He might then be able to see more clearly what must be done. 'In any case, you'll lose a rouble or two if the traffic police see it like this.' I appreciated his advice, especially when he called a man from a nearby shed and told *him* to take Peter Peugeot for another wash-and-brush-up.

The old woman went back to playing with a little boy, and a pretty girl of about eight. Having some chocolates bought on the Danish ship two weeks ago – it seemed months – I went over and shared out the remains, one less carton to litter the back of the car.

The foreman looked at the Peugeot and came out with the usual queries, most too technical for me to answer. Motioning me to lift the bonnet, he noticed my grimy hands and said to George: 'Who is this man?'

He was told: 'An English writer.'

I screwed off the radiator cap to check the water, and pulled out the dipstick to examine the oil level.

'He doesn't look like a writer,' the manager said. 'He's got workman's hands. Writers don't have hands like that.'

'Some do,' George said, 'like this one.'

'Then he's the first I've ever seen.'

A mechanic stripped down the fuses, and looked at the bulbs, and said they were impossible to replace because the Russian ones in stock wouldn't fit. I showed him my kit of spares, but he found nothing suitable there either. 'We'll have to leave it then.' The manager said he was sorry. I thanked him for his trouble, paid for the car wash, and backed out on to the road.

We had strayed from the Intourist route, so it was necessary to get back onto it, and find our way out of the conurbation to the Kiev road. It was soon plain that we were lost, and George made several attempts to talk us on to the right track, but they only confused us more. I trailed a bus for a while, but lost it when we stopped again to ask directions. We bumped along a narrow unmade-up road between blocks of flats and buildings still under construction, the car already looking as if it hadn't felt clean water for a week.

I cursed at time lost, while George pointed to a road ahead, hoping it would lead us out towards Kiev, but it didn't. We trundled behind a slow lorry splashing mud over us from sandy ruts, climbed an embankment, passed a petrol station, and drove through another roadless area of oil drums, until tarmac was under the wheels once more. 'At least Peter Peugeot's enjoying it,' George said. 'Luckily it's strong enough for this sort of terrain.'

After going around in circles (and at least a couple of isosceles triangles) we were in the middle of the city again, but no signs pointed anywhere sensible. Yet I felt more confident, knew we must keep moving, and put on speed, though George was still uneasy, as he needed to be when the next signpost indicated Rostov-on-Don.

'If we take it,' I said, 'we'll be over the Caucasus before we know where we are, smoking a hubble-bubble in Turkey, or having a meal in Persia. Don't worry, though, I can row back to England across the Bosporus.' By instinct I suddenly revved the car's nose on to a loop road that led to the Kiev highway, shown in big letters, but so easy to see we might have looked for it all day. 'You are now leaving Kharkov,' I said in a posh airline voice. 'We shall arrive in Kiev at approximately twenty-hundred hours, so would you kindly fasten your safety belts?'

'There aren't any,' George said.

Which was true. 'Never mind, we'll have a "forty" each, to cheer us along.' From experience we knew that a Monte Cristo lasted forty kilometres, so treated ourselves to a smoke for that distance whenever the mood took us.

The speedometer needle crept up to sixty, seventy, eighty and ninety, and there I held it steady on the wide straight road almost free of traffic, grit flying into the open windows. In 1925 there was an airline service between Kiev and Kharkov, I told George, 'Twice weekly in six-seater Junkers, and the trip took four hours, so what do you say that we try to make it in the same time with our trusty Peugeot?'

'We won't,' he said, 'because we'll stop at the Intourist Hotel in Poltava and have a solid lunch. We'll need it by then.'

The sun came out as if to stay, and I drove between parks and gardens to the centre, a quiet town, and the first with a gay atmosphere not felt so far on our halts.

I'd read of the famous battle near Poltava in 1709, when Peter the Great defeated the Swedish army of Charles XII, and had fun afterwards torturing his prisoners in the Kremlin. Having recovered from the usual calamities of the past the place was now a centre of engineering, with textile factories and food processing plants. It used to be known – before penicillin, I suppose – for the leeches found in ponds and pools of the environs.

The manageress and waitresses at the hotel looked after us well, for on being told we were in a hurry they served an excellent meal within the ten minutes it took us to have a good wash, getting rid of dust and sweat after 363 kilometres since breakfast.

Eight avenues radiated from the circular space in the centre of town but we had taken good note of the one we had come in by, so had no trouble getting out. At the roundabout on the main road people were waiting for a bus, so I stopped to find out if anyone wanted a lift.

A young woman of about thirty got in, dark haired and good looking, with attractively flashing eyes. She said little, except where she wanted to get off, and that she was a schoolteacher. As I stopped for her to alight we were accosted again by a policeman. He wasn't smiling, either, or interested in the make of the car, but was merely doing his job, whatever that was, though we were soon to find out.

I handed out the usual paperwork from the window: passport, insurance certificate, and last night's hotel bill, regretting I hadn't any Danish shipping vouchers to pad out the bundle and increase his confusion. George and the woman showed their identity cards, at which the copper gave a long look to make sure they weren't forged – I supposed – shuffling everything around and peering at each item. 'It'll take days to get to Kiev at this rate,' I said, 'though at least we're giving him the opportunity to earn his wages.'

Our names, and God knew what else, were inscribed into his notebook, which seemed more sinister than on the last occasions. His Cossack face was expressionless and immovable, till he told the girl to stand by the car, with no sign of letting us go. He began to give her some threatening advice, and I wanted to kill him.

He reread his notebook, to make sure all details were correct and George, usually so calm, was as irritated as I was, when he went back to questioning our passenger. 'If the bastard doesn't let us go,' I said to George, as I also got out of the car, 'and send us on our way in the next few minutes, I'll punch his face in. I don't care who he is. He shouldn't torment a woman like that for nothing. What's she saying to him?'

'That she has a husband and two children waiting for her at home, and she must go soon or they won't get fed.' I closed in, to give him a blast of plain English. Ten years in Siberia wasn't a pretty picture in front of my eyes, but what the fuck, it would be something to write a bestseller about. No, I neither thought nor saw, it was just that my wires had burned away.

George, not wanting an international incident, pulled me back. He'd been seconded after all to prevent such a brawl, though he was equally angry for the same gentlemanly reasons. Taking a strong breath to ·reorientate his usual air of soft diplomacy, he said to the policeman: 'This man' – pointing at me – 'is a writer from England. He's a well-known journalist as well, so if you don't turn the woman free, and then us as well, he'll be sure to write a big article about the incident in the foreign press which will go all over the capitalist world, and as for you, you'll end your days earning your pension in the Gulag.'

I didn't know what he was saying in his stern, measured, yet heroically inspired way until he told me later, but the whole thing was over in seconds, well, say half a minute. The policeman immediately shut his notebook, and gave all our documents back. The woman was creased with laughter, but turned away so as not to be seen, while the scared copper tapped her on the shoulder and said she was free to go. He then indicated, with a stiff lip and an exaggerated salute, that we could get back on to the Kiev highway.

Making sure the woman had set off for her nearby village, and hoping the militiaman would crawl into his box and shed bitter tears, I drove at the regulation speed away from the crossroads. 'What was all that for?'

'I'll tell you when my heart stops pounding.' After we had lit our forties he said: 'He was checking up. Maybe he thought the car was stolen.'

I added another expletive to his already extensive collection. 'She won't get into any more trouble because we gave her a lift?'

'Not now.' He told what had been said at the final round, and after a good laugh went on: 'He knows in any case that people are often given lifts by foreign cars. Russians as well, even lorries, anything that happens to come along. There's nothing against it, though I'm mystified as to why we're being stopped so often. Perhaps it's because the car's more foreign than most, but I've been all over Russia with my uncle and we've only ever been pulled in for a good reason. There are foreigners though who deliberately earn roubles by giving lifts, and spending them in the towns.'

I had noticed how people offered a note or two afterwards, though I never took them. Black earth and wooded steppe to either side – all fell back as we sped towards Kiev. For a while the terrain was swampy, then came rich fields of wheat, maize, sunflowers, and sugar beet, a land of plenty where cattle munched their eternal supply of grass, as well as – you could tell by your nose – the famous Mirgorod breed of pigs snouting between wooden houses and the road. At the sound of the car they sometimes ran for the wheels instead of making for safety, and I had also to watch out for children who showed little sense of self-preservation.

I dropped to a crawl in villages because there was no overtaking, sometimes stuck behind a tractor, or a lorry whose trailer was dangerously swaying, making it impossible to get by even on a straight stretch.

Lorries were often stuck in the soft earth, with no local resources, it seemed, to get them upright. Some upended and minus wheels had gone derelict. I supposed that so many were produced it was cheaper to leave them rather than pay the cost of repairs. In any case, they all belonged to the state, so what did it matter?

Signposts to places I had first seen on maps during the war – Dneipropetrovsk, Kremenchug, Cherkassy, Sevastopol – resonated after so much repetition on the Home Service news. The police stopped us again at Lubny for no plain reason I could see, and took our names and the number of the car, a short delay this time. 'If this happens to every tourist motoring through Russia and the Ukraine I can't imagine anybody wanting to come back, what with the hold ups at the frontier as well.'

George was calm again. 'They always do. Perhaps it makes their trip more interesting, and they don't get so angry about it as you.'

'That's because they've led sheltered lives, and think the police are their servants protecting them from the lower orders, but if ever such harrassment became serious in England, with the police trying all the time to crush your spirit, people would unite and take up arms – at least I hope they would. But the world's full of little Hitlers.'

Ever-gallant George made an effort to change my state of mind, by retailing the sexual antics of young Russians during summer vacations on the Black Sea. There was a game, he said, that began by enlisting whatever willing girls could be found. In the largest room they stripped and formed themselves into a 'daisy circle' on the floor, with legs pointing outwards, and made themselves available to the stalwarts who moved, until they couldn't any longer, from one to another.

'I suppose everyone was tanked up with vodka.'

'Oh no, such lovely fun-loving girls wouldn't do it for less than the best Georgian champagne. But I assure you that a good time was had by all.'

'You included?'

'Certainly not,' he laughed.

The car, from going smoothly, slowed down so much that it would obviously stop, possibly in the middle of the road, though I was able to get sufficiently to the right and free from danger. We were out of petrol. 'Now settle the problem, Mr English writer,' said George.

There was suddenly more traffic behind, a black tanker so close to my arse that the driver's mate grinned on overtaking, though before they clipped my tailgate the remaining impetus of the engine got us unscathed on to the muddy verge. 'It's no disaster,' I said, having taken the AA's advice, 'there's a full ten-litre jerrycan behind.'

We disembarked, drank coffee from the flask filled at the hotel in Poltava, and snacked on sandwiches from the same place, standing by the opened back of the car that was beginning to look like the counter of a hotdog stand on Battersea Bridge.

There was, nevertheless, a bereft feeling on being by the roadside with an immobilised car sixty miles from the nearest pump, but I took out the can, and the funnel which I found wouldn't fit unless I could make it go around corners. Petrol, nowhere near the entrance to the tank, went splashing on to the ground. But English fumbling, and Soviet improvisation, finally coaxed most of the fuel in, and off we went.

At the next filling station near Piryatin, I joined the queue, while George went to the office and got a ticket for forty litres. A tall, pink-faced, middle-aged man in baggy shorts stomped from a German car in front. He put out his hand, so we shook, though I didn't know him from Adam, but he greeted me like a brother, and asked in French about my jouney so far, for he was going to Moscow. Seeing the GB sign, he then went over everything again, in English.

A gypsy woman with a baby jabbed me in the ribs, wanting money. George frowned, hoping she would go away. 'They're only gypsies,' I said. My soul delighted at this manifestation of a real live beggar in communist Russia.

An extended family was in temporary occupation of the area, and I hoped they would make a killing before the militiaman came and took their names – or asked for their bloody passports. Swarthy, and beautifully dressed, they came from Bessarabia, mothers, children and one old man, the only bright sparks in this otherwise squalid petrol station. Communism had washed its hands of them, I supposed, but hadn't killed them off as inferior beings as the Germans had tried to do. Here they were left more or less to themselves, though the rapidity of their frequent glances in the direction of the office showed that trouble from the overseer might erupt at any moment. It was like being in Spain rather than on the road to Kiev. I'd heard, mostly from those who had more than enough money to live on, that it was antisocial to give them anything, but I handed over a few of the roubles that couldn't be taken beyond the frontier.

It was pay first then serve yourself. George expertly set the gauge to the amount ordered and pressed the handle. It was as well to know what the tank would take because if you asked for any more a litre or so might splash over your boots, the shine dulled off them forever. But George always got it right.

Seven hundred kilometres out of Kursk, we were approaching the Great Gates of Kiev, at dusk and from the east. Occasional gaps through trees lining the road gave distant views of wooded heights, golden cupolas of churches and monasteries above the vegetation, but no evidence yet as to where the inhabitants lived.

The high right bank of rivers in Russia is always on the western side, meaning that when the invader reaches it there is great difficulty defending the opposite low bank – though at Stalingrad it had to be possible. Such rivers favour the transgressor also when he retreats, the upper ground again on his side. Not that this did the Germans much good in the end, though it was hard luck for the Russians having the natural features against them.

Driving over the handsome new bridge of the grey-green Dneiper, a pinkish sun flushed the golden domes of the churches and coloured the water upstream. It felt as if I had driven well over two thousand miles, and halfway across the Ukraine, for the sake of this astonishing picture. Coming by the back door and into the fading light of Kiev, all other landscapes were forgotten. Beyond the bridge we wondered where the hotel could be, but George did his usual talking act, and we turned right along the treelined road, to the Intourist Hotel on Lenin Street, just off Kreschatchik Boulevard.

Wednesday, 28 June

Well rested by morning, after a breakfast in my room of jellied sturgeon, caviar and boiled eggs, I went to send a few wires at the post office: three to those who had been so helpful in Moscow and Leningrad, and a letter-telegram to London which had been out of my mind since entering Russia.

A previously arranged event was a ten-mile trip by hydrofoil up the Dneiper to its confluence with the Desna. Baedeker's *Russia* of 1914 said you could also steam downriver to the Black Sea, or take a boat northwest via Kalinkovichi to Pinsk and a train to Warsaw. Not any more.

I relaxed on deck, relishing the vistas through binoculars as we moved away from Kiev. Land was flat to starboard, but wooded hills surfed gently west. Our vessel roared its way to the division of the rivers at which, all too soon, it must turn around. A single family in bathing suits gathered for a picnic at a beach of glistening sand.

No need of jackets in the summer warmth, we strolled along wide avenues under the sheltering foliage of great chestnut trees – a magnificent southern city. Young women in their light clothing were a pleasure to observe, though in winter they would be well bundled up, when the temperature went down to minus six centigrade for four months.

George and I called at the bookshops on Lenin Street, and of course I looked for maps. A transport plan of the city showed the layout clearly but, as usual, had no scale. I had dreamlike visions of coming across well-drawn accurate topographical maps, but didn't think I ever would in my lifetime. In another shop I bought Ukrainian silk shirts with embroidered collars.

We had lunch at the Dynamo Restaurant on Kirov Street, starting with borscht and blobs of sour cream. Then came what else but 'chicken à la Kiev' – cutlets of rolled white meat dripping butter. The dish was more delicately cooked than in Russia proper. After cakes and coffee we voted with our feet – or eyelids – for the hotel. More tired than we knew, I slept for several hours.

The most prominent statue in Kiev, after Lenin of course, was of the Cossack hetman Bogdan Khmelnitsky who, from 1648–54 led a war of liberation against Polish rule. He afterwards demanded that Ukraine be annexed to Russia, so was regarded by the tsarist and now the Soviet authorities as a great hero. The town of Proskurov was renamed in his honour in 1954, but as well as slaughtering any Poles he came across, his horde laid waste dozens of Jewish towns and villages, and murdered tens of thousands of their innocent inhabitants. His name was therefore anathema to me, whatever he did for Russia.

A more deserved monument was erected to General Vatutin, in command at the Battle of Stalingrad and the liberation of Kharkov, but mortally wounded at the recapture of Kiev. On the sixteen-foot sculpture of grey granite the simple inscription reads: 'To General Vatutin, from the Ukrainian people.'

In 1941–3 the Germans burned down Kiev University, razed nearly all the buildings around the main boulevards, destroyed the town hall, and dynamited the precious Church of the Dormition. A hundred thousand people were sent to forced labour in Germany, and two hundred thousand others murdered, including over a hundred thousand Jews at Babi Yar, a ravine on the city's outskirts. The massacre was the subject of a poem by Yevtushenko, and described in a novel by Anatoly Kuznetsov.

In the evening I read poetry at the Palace of Culture, and had dinner with other writers and several local officials. The poet Mark Pinchevsky asked about recent writing in England, and told me that David Storey's *This Sporting Life* had recently come out in a Ukrainian translation. The large printing sold in a day, and it was now hard to obtain a copy. The royalties, Mark said, would provide sufficient for Storey to spend a couple of interesting weeks in Kiev, if he got in touch with the Writers' Union.

I said I would pass the information, and did, though I don't think David took advantage of it. Pinchevsky asked if I would send him a copy of *Roget's Thesaurus*, and Hemingway's *For Whom the Bell Tolls*. I agreed to do so.

I don't recall getting to bed that night, but felt no insupportable effects next morning.

Thursday, 29 June
We joined a conducted tour of the Perchersky Lavra and the Monastery of the Caves. Founded on its wooded hill slope above the river in the 11th century, part of its inner acres were set aside for the accommodation of the 150,000 pilgrims up to 1914 who were said to come there every year to the most highly revered convent in Russia.

I had often noted, in a Baedeker bought in a Nottingham bookshop for five shillings twenty years before, the Catacombs of St Anthony in Kiev, and now I could see them. Excavated in clay soil, and supported by masonry, they honeycombed the ground under the cathedral.

Just above six feet in height, only one person at a time could pass along the claustrophobic tunnels. Our serpentine group, provided with candles, was led by a monk, who pointed out the seventy-three saints at peace in their niches, bodies in open coffins mummified due to the benign temperature and chemical properties of the soil. The holy air was stifling, possibly from candle fumes, and in half an hour I was glad to see open sky, and hear the great bell of the Lavra tolling its sombre notes.

After a nap I walked with Mark Pinchevsky to a balustrade overlooking the river, where we talked further about writers and writing. Asking about censorship in the Soviet Union, he said that at present things were much better than they had been, though he wasn't optimistic, because the lid could come down any moment.

He handed me some of his poems, with English versions, and asked if I could get them published in London. I told him about *Modern Poetry in Translation*, a magazine started by Daniel Weissbort and Ted Hughes. I was on the editorial board, and promised to see what could be done. He said I shouldn't say anything about taking his manuscripts out of the Soviet Union, nor let them be seen at the frontier.

At supper in the Intourist Hotel I was presented with a rare and beautiful edition of Shevchenko's poems, the script of his handwriting reproduced on light blue paper, and translated into Russian.

Shevchenko (1814–61) was regarded as 'the father of Ukrainian literature', and his writings were so feared by the tsarist authorities that he was sent to Siberia, and forbidden to write or paint – though he did small drawings whenever his guards were out of sight.

Also at the table was a bald stocky middle-aged man, the only one wearing a suit and tie, who almost pleaded with me to write him a letter soon after my return to London. Shy and introverted, he spoke no English, but at every official gathering he had been so solicitous regarding my well-being that it felt as if he thought he had met me somewhere before but couldn't recall at what place or why, yet was hoping he would have enough time during my stay to find out. We talked as much as was possible with my limited Russian, but I couldn't gather anything about him except that he had some position in the Kiev Writers' Union. I did, however, tell him I would write the letter he wanted.

Friday, 30 June
At half past eight I stood among my hosts outside the hotel so that George and others could take a photograph, the Peugeot waiting impatiently by the pavement. I was fourth from the right, and Igor Petrovich Kasimirov, the man who had been so curious about me the evening before, was on the extreme left.

Done with the handshakes and embraces, among what had come to seem an extended family, George and I located the relevant *chaussée* and were soon free of Kiev. The road to Zhitomir made for easy driving, in clear visibility but under low cloud. After an interesting stay by the Dneiper we nevertheless agreed that being on the road was the life for us. Just before Zhitomir we tanked up with petrol and were then signposted from the town centre, along streets of detached and comfortable houses set in flowered gardens.

Heading south, we lit a forty each, chatting away the miles.

George said that his greatest wish was to come to London, though he daren't imagine that it would ever be possible. He had gathered so much information about the place for his essays on Evelyn Waugh and Oscar Wilde that he already knew the layout, and what it would be like.

'It might not be quite what you think,' I said, 'but when you do get there' – such firm friends had we become – 'you must contact me immediately and come to see us in Clapham, where Wilberforce lived who abolished slavery. I promise there'll be lots of good food, and vodka to drink. The sky will be the limit, and I'll even put a few forties in storage so that we can puff away and talk about old times.'

In Chekhov's *Three Sisters* Chebutykin read from a newspaper, to one of the sisters who deplored the boredom of provincial life, that 'Balzac was happy in Berdichev', so I wanted to see that place.

Balzac spent the whole of 1849 at nearby Verkhovnya, on the estate belonging to Countess Evelyne Hanska. He had been in love with her for sixteen years, and she with him, but they weren't able to marry until her husband had died, when they tied the knot in St Barbara's Roman Catholic church in Berdichev on 14 March 1850.

I also wanted to see the town because it had been 'the religious capital' of Judaism with, by the late nineteenth century, seven synagogues and numerous houses of prayer. Jewish bankers and merchants had invested in the nascent sugar industry, which still thrived under Soviet control.

The place had also been an important trading centre, with four annual fairs for cattle and country produce. By 1939 more than half its population of 62,000 was Jewish, but then the Germans came. I was interested to see what remained of the historic parts, though knew that the main synagogue had been turned into a textile factory.

I explained all this to George. 'Fine,' he said, 'so we'll find the middle, and after looking around have coffee.' When a road on the outskirts forked off for the town, and he indicated that we should go to the right, a resplendent policeman came out of his box and, perhaps guessing our intention, made perfectly understandable motions with his stick that we must stay on the main route. To go through the town, he said when I pulled in, was not on the Intourist itinerary. Nothing had been said in Moscow about it being out of bounds, and George told him so.

'Well it is now,' the policeman smiled. 'So get going.'

I only wished that his box had been horizontal with the ground, and that he was lying in it as dead as dead could be, with a golden rouble weighing down each shuttered eye. I hoped his wife, children, and half a dozen pallbearers would come, hammer the lid of the box firmly into place, and take it away for a long delayed burial at the cemetery.

'He must have been lying. He could easily have let us through,' I said, not even trying to think up more curses for George's list, which in any case was already brimming over. We motored on in silence, I knowing that neither did he think much of unco-operative coppers by now.

We vetoed stopping at Vinnitsa to see the ruins of Hitler's wartime headquarters, but a few miles beyond it seemed time to eat our packed lunch from the hotel. I parked close to a marshy ditch and, remembering the camera, took photos of George scoffing by the car, he then reciprocating with a shot of me, while denying that *scoffing*, at least in his case, could ever be the appropriate description of his way of eating.

Beyond trees across the road a high official-looking fence was visible, maybe of an airfield at Ivcha, near Litin, I decided, looking at the relevant sheet of my secret map. George was dubious but said nothing, having seen me do it a few times before, when I told him we needed to check the navigation.

A covered lorry went by at cruising speed. Well, they sometimes did. Even the aerial on top seemed no strange thing, but a few minutes later – as I was searching for the overseas frequency on my radio to get the news – the same vehicle came slowly back, and parked a couple of hundred yards beyond. 'Perhaps we'd better get going,' George said.

The BBC wouldn't come through, for the batteries were all but run down, so we packed up just as the lorry came trawling back.

Our feckless selves again, we calculated how many roubles we'd be to the good if some benign authority presented us with one after every mile done. Totting them up since Leningrad, we changed the amount into pounds, then dollars, and switched the whole sum back into roubles while smoking another forty. A variant on the game was that when I overtook a car we awarded ourselves ten roubles, and fifty for a lorry. 'How can we not make money, smoking such cigars?' George laughed, acting the plutocrat with delight.

When I said we were making a lot of Monopoly money he wanted to know about the game, and after explaining I went on to say that in England, if not the whole of the Western world, it had always been the favourite pastime of young would-be capitalists. He was appalled when I said that even children took to it with avidity. Not only that, but the Bolshevik leaders in the 'twenties and 'thirties played it behind locked doors in the Kremlin. Stalin loved it, and had a special Russian version made, but someone playing with him had the temerity to cheat.

He must have been full of vodka, but Stalin had him arrested, and it was that which set off the purges.

A brigade of Red Army tanks was crossing the road, and the general who leaned out of his staff jeep had a fit when I stopped to watch the spectacle from close by, which was like a scene from the movies, or a page out of *The Volga Rises in Europe* by Curzio Malaparte.

His big face turning purple at the sight of our foreign number plates, as if I might report on the manoeuvres when back in London, he screamed at us to get moving and out of the way. George, who told me that his language had been worse than any he had heard in his life, thought we had better do so, and I did as well, in case he ordered a tank to nudge us off the road, or even blow us clear with a well-aimed shell. 'They don't fuck about in the Red Army,' George added, so I revved up and got well out of it.

Beyond Proskurov – Khelmnitsky – the day turned hot and sultry, but there wasn't much traffic. A hundred yards or so into the steppe two windmills appeared, unused and lonely, neither man nor bird anywhere. When we stopped I hoped one of the arms at least would creak and start moving under the metallic sky.

Each mill had six sails holed in several places, and if turning they would almost have brushed the soil. Their towers were squat, not in good condition, and a short distance away was a large recently built shed with three doors. Telegraph wires ran along the road, but the only sound broaching the silence was the click of my camera.

The photograph developed in London showed three men sitting by one of the lower sails. They were unmistakably smiling at the camera, so why hadn't I noticed them? Well, neither had George. I'd been sure no one was about, unless my eyes had been so attuned to the road they had grown black patches momentarily – which was unlikely. It was eerie nevertheless, for if anyone had been there I would surely have spotted them, wouldn't I? The photograph said it hadn't lied, so who, or what, was right?

I was as close to Ulashkovtsy – or Loshkovitz, my mother-in-law's birthplace – as I could have been. 'Only a hundred kilometres, a mere bagatelle,' I said to George, 'though it might as well be five hundred, since it's out of bounds. She will certainly be disappointed. What say we light off in that direction, and let the devil take the hind legs? Sturdy old Peugeot can hump along very well on dirt roads, and we can steer by the compass.'

He put on a languid mock upper-class English drawl: 'My dear fellow, I won't encourage you, because I know you'll never make it. We might even come across those tanks again. They travel awfully fast.'

Kamenets Podolski, a picturesque town, had been given two hotels by Baedeker, but we missed both, even supposing they still existed. After slowly crossing a Turkish bridge over the River Smotrich we took photographs of the rearward view, churches and a monastery high above the ravine and surrounding trees.

'Only another hundred kilometres and we'll be in Chernovtsy.' George looked up from the map. 'And it's our last day together, my friend. How very sad for me.'

'The same for me as well, old pal.' We went over the Dneister at Khotin, and soon afterwards turned westerly through fertile country with many villages. An agglomeration of houses on a hill to the right near Chernovtsy signified Sadagora, another great centre of Jewish Hassidism. The place was marked on the large scale Austrian staff map, but George didn't consider that spy material because it was so out of date.

I noticed a sandy bathing place, before turning to cross the Pruth and trundling up the main street. We found our hotel easily, for it stood prominently on the same thoroughfare. According to the AA the day's tally had been 351 miles.

After a wash and change we went for a six o'clock stroll towards the river to exercise our legs. Chernovtsy, or Czernowitz, was the nearest stop to my mother-in-law's birth-place, so I carried the camera to get a few shots of the streets and typical houses which she might have known, little of their aspect having changed since her day.

George said I shouldn't take pictures in the town, and I wanted to know why, refusing to worry whether or not my behaviour would figure in his obligatory report when he got back to Moscow. 'Is it because a few of the houses are a bit run down? Or that there are bridges, barracks and airfields in the vicinity? I can't see any. I'm only an innocent tourist wanting to record memories of the surroundings, and if the authorities have any objection they can take a running jump at themselves.'

I explained the meaning of 'running jump', or tried to and so, not holding anything against me, he was good natured enough to say no more, while I went on clicking at balconies and façades.

At our farewell dinner we talked again, over vodka and then champagne, about the possibility of his coming to London. 'The sooner the better. I'll be waiting for you.' In the morning he would set out on a 24-hour journey to Moscow, while I would make my way to the Rumanian frontier, only one Monte Cristo in distance. I agreed to this short lap on my own, because if he came with me he might not get his train till the following day. He wanted to hasten back to the arms of his girlfriend, and who could blame him? 'I hope the tears are dry on her blouse by the time you get there.'

I made sure he had enough cigars for the journey, and promised to send books from London as soon as possible. The Ost Europa map used on the trip was sufficiently clean for me to leave as a gift for his uncle.

Saturday, 1 July

While packing his case in the hotel room after breakfast, and contemplating the long and roundabout route to Moscow, the telephone rang, as I was told by George much later.

A stern male voice exploded into the earpiece: 'This is Colonel Burdenko (let's call him). I'm glad I've found you at last. You're in very serious trouble, Comrade Andjaparidze. Is it true that yesterday you were in the car of a foreign spy, who was observed looking at maps, taking photographs, and working a radio while parked close to the military aerodrome at Ivcha? I don't want any of your lies, so be careful what you say. At the moment I'm making a report on the matter, but thought it better for us to talk before having you arrested. Explain yourself, if you can.'

George was shocked at the colonel's screed, and had visions, even though innocent, of never seeing mother, aunt, or girl-friend again, or at least not before returning from a ten-year stretch in some prison beyond the Urals. Maybe they would even have him shot.

He told the colonel that the stop had been at that particular place only by coincidence. The Englishman had seen space at the roadside and decided to pull in because we were hungry and had to eat. The English writer had looked at the map to find out how many miles we were from Chernovtsy.

The colonel broke in: 'That's a lie and you know it. It's impossible. You don't try to find out a fact of that sort unless you're at a crossroads, or in a town where there are signposts. Don't try to deceive me, or it will turn out very bad for you. And the radio, what do you say about that?'

George wondered if the man was joking, or if he was a hoaxer, yet knew it couldn't be when the colonel shouted at his carelessness and unpatriotic lack of vigilance in having co-operated with a potential enemy who wanted to snoop – with a camera as well – on military installations.

With many reiterations George said that neither of us had known there was an airbase in the area. Employing all his diplomatic charms, which meant a good deal of vocal kow-towing, he was finally able to calm the conversation by reminding the colonel that the road was, after all, on the specified Intourist route, and that many foreign cars (including German cars) passed the aerodrome without knowing it to exist. 'We only stopped to eat, and we wouldn't have done so if we had known.'

Not even a fiery colonel could doubt George's innocence for long. 'All right. I'll try to get you off the hook, but don't ever let anything like that happen again. You're old enough to know that we have to be careful about security.'

I had left the hotel at nine and knew nothing of that at the time. I drove up to the central square, the old Austrian Ringplatz, which seemed already in another country, not having the dimensions of those in Russia or the Ukraine, with their vast open fields of fire in case of an insurrection.

The square was homely, and small, and trams rattled around

like toys in Hamley's window, so Austrian I looked for a confectioner's, where I could linger over a *sachertorte* with coils of cream to go with the coffee – a dream, because such availability had long since gone, and stay I couldn't, for the urge was on me to quit Russia as soon as possible.

Without Tovarich George for company, I took the wrong road – that fatal left turning again – and ended up in the outskirts, near squalid decrepit houses on an unpaved lane. A gaggle of untidy children and their mothers looked on as I did a quick three-point manoeuvre over the ruts, and went back to find the proper route.

It took little time to reach the border, where I was stalled – if that's the word – and only wanted to get into Rumania and reach the open road of days in Russia. Meanwhile I attended to my notebook, which helped me to be patient.

Four cars were in front, but the customs officers and frontier police more than took their time. They went so thoroughly over each one that God knew – again – what they were looking for and how much longer the wait would take. It was the reverse performance of getting in from Finland, so I resigned myself to losing half a day.

It was as hot as an oven, and I didn't envy the fractious children who filled one of the cars in front. A wind howled through the heat, shimmering across nearby woods on its way to sear the fair fields of the Bukovina. Even wheel hubs were being taken off and sniffed. Was it gold, currency, drugs, or icons – the usual questions. Perhaps they'll suck oil from the engines, or drain the petrol tanks. All I had was the usual tourist's stuff, and as for Mark Pinchevsky's bundle of poems, they were snug in the holdall pocket with my survey maps.

Czernowitz had always been in a region of shifting frontiers between the Baltic and the Black Sea, shuttlecocked and battledored from Austrians to Russians to Rumanians and back again. Laden wagons in the fifteenth century probably took longer to cross when it was a customs post of Moldavia.

People were saying goodbye to a Ukrainian family in their Volkswagen Estate, everyone jolly enough except for an old woman wiping tears away with the corner of a headscarf at seeing them – so I hoped – about to depart. Perhaps they had once lived in Chernovtsy and, on becoming displaced as a result of the war, had prospered in Germany, and were now allowed to come back and visit relatives. Two Skodas with Polish number plates drove in from the other side and, if from Warsaw, must have spent a week crossing borders.

Scribble, scribble, the notebook saved me. I wrote about an imaginary country even more difficult to get into and out of than this one. Nihilism would be the policy of the ruling party, with confusion indescribable (almost) and yet the plot of the novel to be written one day would move on the experiences of six people sent to Nihilon to gather data for a Baedeker-style guidebook. Thus no wait is wasted.

Two hours later I was signalled through, which wasn't so long after all. I had grumbled, though only to myself. The gate into *terra incognita* was opened by a soldier, and I was in Rumania. He indicated that I stop, get out, and wash my hands thoroughly at a tap and bowl surreally in the open air by the side of the track. I did so, using the clean towel provided. I was further amused when told to drive the car on to a large square covered with sawdust, where another soldier with a canister on his back sprayed all four wheels and underparts of the chassis with strong disinfectant. I was glad he didn't squirt the stuff over my boots as well.

After the cleansing procedure a tall queenly woman in a grey, well-cut dress over her equally queenly bosom, with dark upswept hair as if it had been coiffured only that morning at the best salon in Bucharest, trod her careful way from the police and customs building and, when I told her how long I had waited to be admitted in to her lovely country, said in good English: 'That's Soviet Russia for you. What can you expect from them?'

She took my passport, visa, and car insurance papers, and in a very short time brought them back all stamped and approved, then showed where to change a ten-pound traveller's cheque, before leading me to a buffet for a good sustaining lunch. Charmed by her helpfulness, I gave her a signed copy of one of my books in Rumanian, which she graciously received. She would have preferred one in English, perhaps, but I didn't have one, and she was far too well bred to say anything. At a souvenir shop I bought some embroidered peasant blouses for my sisters, and a wooden musical shepherd's pipe with 'Bukovina' burned along the side.

Sensing the liberty of open spaces, Peter Peugeot, with a backward nod to George no longer with us, went like a greyhound into beautiful Rumania. At Siret I turned him southwest on to Road 17A, and climbed smoothly into the Carpathian Mountains, the main physical obstacle before the Danube at Belgrade.

The paving ceased, though the road was dry and well engineered, enough for a fair speed to be maintained on upward curves through spruce and pine forests.

Already back in the Balkan part of Central Europe, the mountain air was sweet, and geology under the car gave a firm tread. Roman legions had got this far, so I was culturally nearer home.

The mind emptied enough for me to give sharp attention to the road. Most agreeably, I was without thought of a final destination, as if free to go for ever from one pleasant and unexplored locality to another, the Wandering yet undriven Jew, having the wherewithall to keep moving for eternity. Rumania seemed the country to do it in after such humane treatment at the frontier, as well as being in an alpine region better on the eyes than the unending flatness of the Ukraine.

The car was aimed only as far as the next bend, and I refused to imagine the terrain beyond till I got there. For long it was the same, and that was how I liked it. The weather was good, though the sky laid down a roof of low amorphous cloud, and I thought that if it rained I would be scooting through a sea of red mud.

A German Mercedes full of people and with a perilously laden roofrack came towards me as if about to take one of the hairpin bends. It was, and I got well into the side to let it by. The only car I'd seen for many miles, it slithered on the turn and, thinking it might hit a rock, I did a rapid rundown of what first aid I knew, but whoever was at the wheel came back on course, and arrowed his way towards the frontier hoping, I supposed, to get to Chernovtsy by nightfall. I wished him luck with a wave he wouldn't have noticed.

The covered slopes lifted 4,000 feet on either side, though I had little idea of my height above sea level. The air became cooler so I stopped to put on a jacket.

On a short straight stretch at the col a man stood as if to see me safely over. I took him at first to be a shepherd caring for a few sheep seen earlier. He was moustached and middle aged, a dignified statue formally and locally dressed, wearing smart boots and leggings, and a blanket folded neatly over his chest as if he had been a soldier in younger days. The Tyrolean-style hat had a little green feather up the side, and he held himself as if owning the land around, his stance that of a gamekeeper, or the steward of a gentleman's estate, though I supposed there were no such in present-day Rumania. As I slowed down to go by he gave a smart and studied salute, which I had time to acknowledge.

I crossed one branch of the range, then went down to a village, the road going between the backs of squalid wooden houses. The surface was so cut up I feared that even the sturdy Peugeot might get stuck in one of the muddy ruts, but I was soon on a more viable surface and ascending to another pass of over a thousand metres.

As the afternoon lengthened, and on joining the main road at Vatra Dornei, I wondered where to spend the night. A finger post pointed a few miles back to Cimpulung, which had a spa hotel providing mud baths, but I already felt muddy enough, and decided to press on for sixty more miles to Bistrita.

This meant an ascent by more unpaved road to the col of Tihuta, of 1,227 metres. By then I was accustomed to mountain driving, having in any case done much in Spain. The road descended to the banks of the quick flowing Bistrits, on its way to join the Szamos, eventually reaching the Black Sea via Belgrade.

The road brought me to a village of good houses, showing every sign of prosperity. Crowds gathered around a gypsy band of five lithe young men wearing hats and suits. Maybe it was part of a wedding celebration, for everyone was smiling and entranced in a festival area spilling on to the road.

They were steamed up for revelry, and it was Saturday night, most of them in traditional costume, young women wearing the sort of blouses I'd bought at the frontier. Pausing a moment at such lively music, I wondered what would happen if I got out of the car and began highstepping among those already on the hop. But I was tired, and would of course have made a fool of myself, no longer having the cool advice of George to deter me. The people would no doubt have been hospitably amused had I done so, filling myself up with the local wine which had a reputation of being as good as the famous Tokay.

At dusk I drove into Bistrita, an old Saxon town founded in the twelfth century, with a Gothic protestant church in the market place. My Baedeker of *Austria–Hungary* said that a few miles northwest was a castle that had been destroyed by the townsfolk in 1465, and I suddenly remembered that I had fallen on the very place – Bistrita – where Jonathan Barker spent the night before calling on Count Dracula, though whether he stayed in the same simple one-star hotel I was walking towards with an overnight bag on my shoulders there was no way of knowing.

On showing my passport at the counter a frowsty middle-aged woman in a black dress gave me a form to fill in, instructing me how to do so in an unmistakable New York accent. 'You're on your own?' she asked with surprise and disapproval, seeing me write in the appropriate square that I was married. 'So where's your wife?'

I wondered what bloody business it was of hers, but told her she was at home.

Her voice rose plangently: 'You mean to say you're travelling without your wife?' If I had known what was coming I would have lied on completing the form. 'And how many weeks is it since you've seen her?'

I was abashed, though determined to feel no shame. On the other hand I was amused. 'About three weeks.'

She shuffled away, shaking her head. 'A man come all this way, without his wife!'

When she returned I asked, as a diversion, where she had learned such excellent English. 'Don't ask!' she said, glad I had. 'I lived in America a long time, but came back here.' More than that she wouldn't say, went grumbling into the kitchen to tell one of Dracula's minions called Boris to start work on my supper.

I walked around the gloomily lit market place, where a few disgruntled men at a café table followed my progress. I would have sat for a drink but needed to exercise my legs that had stiffened from the constant changing of gears on mountain roads. In any case I didn't want to run into anyone else in case they berated me in English for travelling without my wife.

I sat in the hotel dining room for half an hour before tall gormless Boris slouched in to serve supper. Being the only guest, it was as if I had landed there to be eaten instead of to eat. The basic repast of rice, meat and vegetables was welcome, but best of all was a bottle of fiery red wine which, in not too long, sent me upstairs and knocked me into sleep with the subtlety of a rubber hammer, bringing dreams of endless alpine roads patrolled by lovely beckoning girls in braids and embroidered blouses.

I was only 240 kilometres from Chernovtsy, but the day had been long, and all I knew was that I had found my way through the Carpathians, the longest mountain range in Europe.

Sunday, 2 July
Breakfast, I said to myself, is the most important meal for me. Then I wasn't sure. All were vital while motoring, an occupation good for the appetite, I knew, as Boris came in with

a smile (he too must have slept well) a dish of pale delicious butter, fresh breads, a pot of kitchen-made jam, and all the coffee I could drink, a spread which could not I was sure have been bettered at the higher grade establishment in Cimpulung, mud bath thrown in or not. She who had chastened me for not having brought the family to see the unique marvels of Transylvania noted my feeding with satisfaction. In her Rumanian fashion she was concerned for my well-being, and we were friendly on saying goodbye.

Before nine I was making westerly back on Route 17. Signposts saying Beclean beckoned me, taken in as *Be Clean*, though I was nothing less after a coolish morning shower in the hotel. The road dipped south to avoid a 2,000-foot spur, then northerly and west again through the villages of Sieul Maghorus, Sieul Sfantu and Sintareay – I think I spell them correctly.

At Beclean, turning right over the river (back on AA instructions after the road of yesterday), I bore left and threaded other settlements to Dej, with its Calvinist church and nearby salt mines.

It was my second day of solo driving since Leningrad, and I was beginning to enjoy it, with all of vast Rumania before me. There was no majordomo to overlook my idiosyncratic style of motoring, or to blushingly forgive strings of obscene complaint. No one knew or cared where I was going, and I liked that. No one worried about my behaviour, as in Russia. The elegant woman at the frontier had already turned her benevolent attentions on other travellers, and forgotten my transit, and the Rumanian police who had registered my entry were sufficiently human and slapdash not to be interested in my whereabouts.

The illusion of freedom to roam was almost overwhelming.

Thanks to the Ancient Romans all signs were in Western script, and I had even figured the headlines of a newspaper in the hotel, with the help of French or Spanish. The country was surrounded by languages I didn't understand, but Rumanian could be made sufficiently plain on requesting food, coffee or car fuel, though sometimes with the help of the *aperçu linguistique* in the *Guide Bleu*. I also read for the first time, while draining my morning coffee, the booklet from the Rumanian tourist office, which stated in English that the speed limit for towns was fifty kilometres an hour, and in the countryside a maximum of eighty. I would therefore need to watch out for the police, though a few local madcaps sometimes overtook me at a greater rate.

I stopped now and again to make out the names of natural features around me, spreading the two sheets of the War Office one-million-scale maps and matching them together on the bonnet. They showed nearly all of Rumania, and gave a superb topographical picture of the great layer-tinted horseshoe of the Carpathians. My route was out of the two prongs, leading to lower areas of mostly light green between Bistrita and the Danube. Widespread landscape was a pleasure to behold, fulfilling the dreams of liberty I had come away to experience.

There was still no safe way, however, of signalling on over-taking cars, lorries or horsedrawn carts, or when turning left and right, but I was accustomed to the problem, and such pains taking caution was an advantage when applied to other manoeuvres, which helped to keep me out of trouble.

The road avoided all heights on going south by following the river and railway to Cluj. After that place the route went on to bare and more hilly terrain as far as Turda, an industrial city of 40,000 inhabitants. Various shades of smoke would, on weekdays, rise from the glass works, cement and chemical factories. Again there were salt mines in the vicinity, and I hoped to be forgiven on wondering who worked in them.

Then it was up and across an empty plateau, before rejoining road and railway winding along the River Mures. It was an area producing good wine, but unfortunately I wasn't able to stop and drink any.

Beyond Alba Julia – more evidence of the far-reaching Romans – I turned west, again by rail and river, and came to Deva, with its medieval fortress. Three hundred kilometres on the trip meter suggested it was time for a meal. The two-star restaurant Perla, in the Filemon Sibu Park, looked suitable because food was served in the open air. Fish was on the menu but, being at least 300 miles from the sea, I chose spicy minced meat and rice rolled in cabbage leaves, and ice cream for dessert.

Two jean-clad white-shirted young men in their twenties asked permission to sit with me. Dredging words up from several languages I told them where I had come from and the way I would be going. The sturdy Russian camera lay by my elbow less to take photographs than to have it before my eyes. One of the men picked it up, sighted it, felt the weight in his palm, and brushed his spotless handkerchief across the lens, meanwhile saying something I didn't understand to his companion.

He laid the camera down, and took an impressive pack of banknotes from his back pocket: 'You want to sell it?'

Perhaps they usually talked to obvious foreigners on the off chance of doing a little business, but it was the first time on the trip anyone had offered to buy one of my belongings. I had been led to expect it in Russia, but no one had asked to buy my clothes, probably because they weren't the fashionable Western sort. Nor had my fountain pen or radio interested anyone.

Had I intended staying longer in Rumania I might have taken up their offer, since the camera was unreliable, a roll of film now and again returning blank from the developers for no reason I could think of. But since I had no need of extra currency, and any that remained could not be taken from their country, there was no reason for a deal.

On my polite refusal they stood, shook my hand, and went away. After coffee and a smoke I called the waitress and asked for the bill, but she laughed and said the men who had been talking to me had settled it already. It was embarrassing, since I wouldn't be seeing them again, so I could only appreciate their generosity, and leave it at that.

Rather than follow Route 68 from Deva I turned more directly to Lugos on the 68B, through Faget, cutting out a wide bend to the south. The mostly unpaved road put the Peugeot on its mettle, me relishing the many lurches and bumps in sidetracking sections that were being improved, though no workmen were present because it was Sunday. I supposed Michelin would have given it a scenic green band, for mountains of over 4,000 feet lay to the right, and as ever on seeing alpine woodlands I thought how pleasant to wander in such an area for a few weeks with rucksack, map, and good boots – a typical fantasy from a speeding car.

Lugos, a textile town, set me wondering whether one of my favourite childhood filmstars Bela Lugosi had been born there, or taken his name from it. Going south from Timisoara, I was soon within breaching distance of the frontier. In an hour or so it would be dusk, and sensible to pass a second night in Rumania, but the magnet of Serbia pulled me along. From the border another hundred kilometres – a short hop in the frame of things – would see me in Belgrade, though I must find a bed before getting trapped in a large strange city at night.

Leaving Rumania was as easy as entering. A policeman strolled out of the office and looked at my passport, sneering in English: 'And you only came into our beautiful country yesterday? You should spend more time with us.'

I lied in telling him I had a schedule to keep, though in truth it didn't much matter when I got to England. 'I'll be sure to come again soon.'

'I hope so.' He stamped my documents with a smile, and saluted. 'Bon voyage!'

I entered Yugoslavia without delay, and called at the money-changing post for a few thousand dinars. A manic foolishness invariably took me over at the end of long drives. Wanting to cover just that few extra miles, I was unable to stop, too cosily boxed into the Peugeot and unwilling to pitch myself among other human beings.

I soon realised there would be little chance of a bed before Belgrade. At Vrsac – I tried saying it but couldn't – there was no accommodation, so in the failing light I took the right fork to Pancevo. No lodgings there, either.

It was clear that I would be lured into the sprawling agglomeration of Belgrade. I crossed the Danube in darkness, so did not see the river. The main throughway on my simplified town plan promised to be broad and clear, and signified a quick way out. It wasn't a spectacularly lit city, but the continuous dazzle of traffic half blinded me. In trying to find a way leading to the Sarajevo exit I became utterly lost. Too late I recalled my firm rule of never negotiating a foreign city in the dark. Such a traverse was bad enough in daylight, but at night everything was uncertain, even perilous, and navigation soon went out of the window.

I travelled up and down, and around main streets (and lesser ones) for miles without spotting any intelligible signpost, so badly worn were my eyes by the lights of cars coming the other way and others flashing from behind, till it seemed I would never reach open country.

The AA routing had ended at the Danube, I couldn't think why, though it would have been little help, and it was no use consulting the fold-out plan in the *Guide Bleu* because I'd never be able to find exactly where I was on it, even street names stuck where it was impossible to see them from a moving car.

I was exhausted, and considered pulling into a quiet street to doze for an hour, but there were no such streets, and to do so seemed an unwarranted defeat. Persistence would finally bring success.

I could have looked for a hotel, but by now had lost the desire to overnight in such a city. I would only wake up with almost the same problem, though in any case didn't see one on my futile zipping here and there like a dying bluebottle at the end of summer. All I could do was stamp on despair and resume my reconnaissance of the town.

Spherical bulbs on lamp posts appeared, white heat against black, crowds walking from a park gate towards waiting buses, talking of what had been heard at a concert. Men and girls, they seemed happy and serious in their shirtsleeves and summer dresses. They made an island of the car when I stood outside it to ask the nearest route out of town. I didn't even care if it led back to Rumania.

An intelligent youth who stopped to light a cigarette indicated at my question that I should reverse the car, go right at the street, join the next main road, and again turn right, which would take me on to a bridge over the Sava.

Where the road went he didn't say, and I didn't ask, only wanting to get unstuck from a trap I had so stupidly fallen into. I made him repeat the explanation, determined to get it right, by which time the multitude around us had dispersed.

I did a three-point turn, and in ten minutes had crossed the specified bridge without a glance at the river. The highway went northwest, and in the suburbs came a signpost for Zagreb, hardly the place to head for, but there would be a turn-off for Sabac in not too long – I knew – where a hotel would put me up for the night. The road was dark and narrow, though well paved. On my various maps it was shown as a motorway, except the more accurate one in the *Guide Bleu*.

I overshot the turn for Sabac and the road to Sarajevo but, having at least noticed it, swung back and drove the last thirty kilometres. Beyond the bridge into town a single light glimmered on a few tables outside the hotel. Well after ten o'clock, I went in to register, hoping it wasn't too late for supper and a bottle of wine. I needn't have worried. There had been a longitudinal time change in my favour after crossing the frontier.

The manager smiled, I supposed, at my raddled appearance, and said a meal would be served outside as soon as it could be made ready, at which good news he took off his jacket, put on a chef's apron, and went to do something in the kitchen.

Relieved, happy, and as light headed as if every hundred kilometres that day had been rewarded with a double vodka, I sat with legs sprawled and smoked a pipeful. The half hour's wait was whiled away by the approach of a slim dark-haired young man who asked, having seen the plates on the car a few yards away by the pavement, if I was English. I told him that, as far as I knew, I was. Wine was set before me, and I invited him to sit down and have a drink, relaxed enough even to share all I owned with the Devil, while knowing I could always call up another bottle.

He thanked me, and said no. 'I would just like to chat with you for a while, if you don't mind, so that I can practice my English.'

He was so fluent I told him he hardly needed to. He said he taught the language at a local school, then wanted to know what I did for a living. On giving lifts in England I always claimed to be a land surveyor, knowing enough on the subject, because I didn't want to fend off questions as to what kind of novels I produced, and how did inspiration come to me etc etc.

Perhaps the day's work had made me more friendly, and I told him I was a writer. His name was Novak, he said, and we talked about life in England, and what sort of books were being published there these days. He had read novels by Jane Austen and Charles Dickens, among others, which gave more to talk about. With half the bottle gone I no longer felt I had driven far, so could chat amicably with him. He informed me that he led a lonely life in Sabac, being a teacher, for it was a rather dull town.

When the meal of steak, fried potatoes and salad was laid on my table he stood, but before going asked if I would kindly post one of my novels to him. I agreed to do so, and doubled back a notebook for him to write:

Mr Novak Pantic,
Sabac-Majur,
Yugoslavia

As an address it seemed brief, but maybe he was well known in the town. I sent him a paperback, and hope he received it.

At midnight by Bistrita time I went to bed, recalling on my way to sleep the concerned landlady at the hotel, which now seemed in another world. My wheels had sliced off northwest Rumania, and I was well over a hundred miles into Serbia, after a run of 700 kilometres, a fair score, but what was the hurry? Even so, it had been a long day, and though it wasn't to be the most I had driven in one 24-hour period (the emerging French motorway system allowed more) it seemed quite enough. A younger man might have merely dined in Sabac, and reached Sarajevo in time for morning coffee, but I wasn't in a race and, having nothing to prove, decided to take things easy from then on.

Monday, 3 July

Three mighty rivers were behind me: the Dneiper, the Dneister, and the Danube. Having crossed the Sava at Sabac, the Drina was next.

Sleep had been deep and long enough, and little time was lost in getting back on the road – though with no sense of haste. After motoring through well-cultivated land, with sparse traffic, came the toil of many curves in the gorge of the Drina. A long stretch of unpaved road beyond the bridge at Dvornik was taken in good spirit by the car.

On pulling into a wayside caravanserai at half past ten I sat outside the main door by a well-used chicken yard. The rustic table I'd been pointed to wobbled enough to be genuine, though I couldn't imagine anyone wanting to buy it even at the top end of the Portobello Road. The liquid was hot and fragrant, and the man who served it seemed as happy as if seeing his first customer of the day.

After a bend in the road, feeling guilty perhaps at having so much space to myself, I drew in to offer three people a lift. There had been no trace of buses so far, but in any case it would save their fares should one miraculously come along.

The tall smartly dressed old man was as aloof and dignified as if I had appeared in exactly the car he had ordered, and that it had arrived a little too late for his liking. By his side, though not too close, a soberly dressed woman held the hand of a pretty young girl garbed in a kind of bridesmaid's outfit. She may have been on her way to be married, but how could I ask? Playing the chauffeur, I got out, cleared the back seat, and saw them ceremoniously installed.

I wondered how to know when they wanted to alight. Perhaps I wouldn't notice the imperative tap on my shoulder till we were beyond the Channel, and the grim immigration minions of officialdom ushered them to the pen for sending back – and me to prison for trying to smuggle them in.

Much I cared, but after fifty kilometres the old man's tone told me we had come to the drop-off point, an isolated spot almost identical to the wooded area where I had taken them on board. I opened the door to let them out on the safe side. There was little traffic, but the occasional passing car always seemed in a blinding hurry to get to Sarajevo.

The old man shook my hand, and asked by putting a finger to his mouth, and pointing to an upgoing track towards a clump of houses, whether I wouldn't like to go with them for food and drink, of which there would be plenty.

When in similar sign language I indicated that the ship must go on, he shook my hand again, and spoke his appreciation of the lift in what I supposed to be Serbo–Croat, though I couldn't be sure, for I may already have been in Bosnia-Herzogovina.

By Lake Baikal in May 1964.

George Andjapasidze, on the road, June 1967.

Full of food by the military installation, unnoticed.

Outside the Writer's Club in Moscow, 1967.

Goodbye Kiev. The man on the right is the one who wanted to know all about me, 1967.

Speaking my mind, Moscow Gorki; Literary Institute, 1967.

A street in Czernowitz. The town on the hill behind is Sadagora, once a great Jewish religious centre, 1967.

Looking back on Kamenets Podolski, 1967.

From Moscow to the South on annotated map.

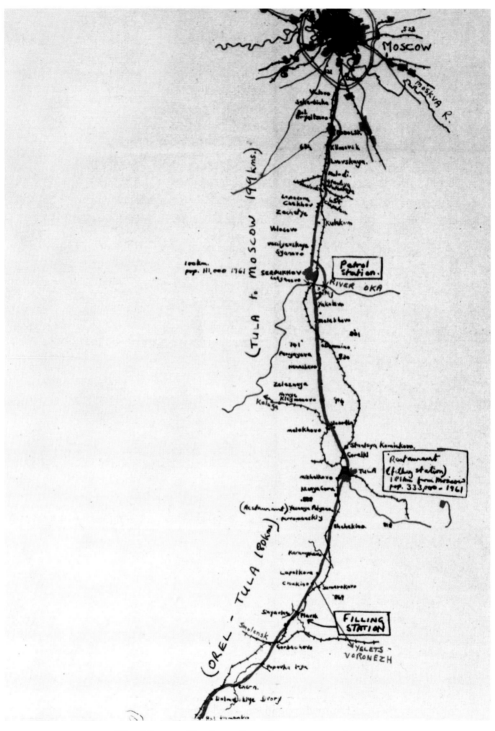

The Moscow-Kursk section of my annotated map.

On to Kursk.

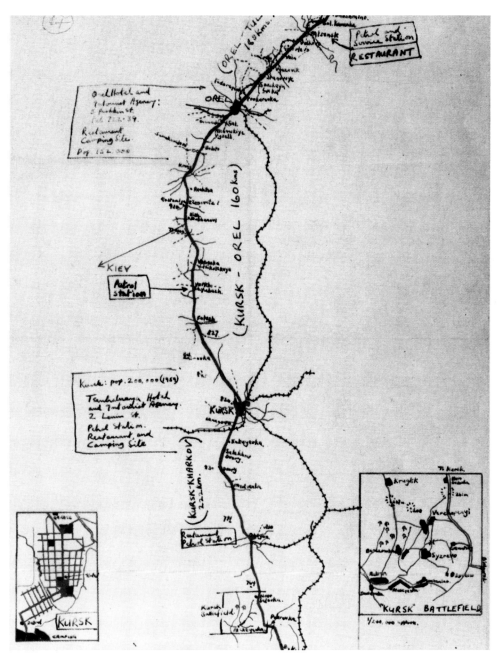

On my home-made, hand-copied map.

10 мая (вторник) 21.00

Встреча с классиком британской литературы **Аланом Силлитоу**

В **19.00** состоится показ фильма Тони Ричардсона "**Одиночество бегуна на длинную дистанцию**" (1962) по сценарию Аллана Силлитоу (без перевода)

by CDP **МУЗЫКАЛЬНЫЙ КЛУБ**
ул. Покровка, 47, м. "Курская", "Красные ворота"
http://cdp.artforus.ru тел. 917-90-70

An announcement of my poetry reading, organised by the British Council in 2005.

The woman also thanked me, while the pretty girl, who had so far not cared to be noticed, gave a smile which might have become a kiss had she not been so firmly chaperoned.

Time was spent, and much fine scenery went by, in regretting that I had not taken the invitation and gone to the feast. I heard the plink of sonorous zithers, and saw dancing in which I would, sooner or later, inevitably have taken part. There would have been unlimited slivovitz, with salted fish and soured cream, platters of saffroned rice, and tender gobbets of skewered lamb. I would have passed a couple of nights wrapped in my sleeping bag on a veranda, smelling the mountain air from one direction, and the smouldering embers of cookfires from another. Who knew what romantic adventures would have come my way, and taught a few poetic words of the language?

Such bucolic revels were not for me, but having let the imagination live them, what more could I want? As consolation it was as good as the real thing which too often fades more quickly. Thus my sense of deprivation was erased.

The car dragged me on, and close to Tuzla but not in it I followed the diverted road directly south. Tuzla was a salt-mining centre (how much did they use in the Balkans?) the word *tuz* being Turkish for that commodity, as I read in Grandma *Blue Guide* on stopping for a call of nature.

The valley curved through wooded country, then the road went up and over a watershed, to rejoin river and railway. At midday I stopped at a primitive coffee shop among the minarets of Sarajevo. For the price of a few dinars I ordered minute but pungent cups, with a plate of teeth-achingly sweet *baklava*, familiar from living in Morocco. The combination raised my senses to a higher state of awareness for driving.

I was out of Europe, for a while, a not disagreeable change as

I relaxed with a cigar, and watched people going about their lives. The town seemed far more easygoing than many other places of equal size.

It hadn't always been because, as every schoolboy knows, or did at one time, the Austrian Archduke Franz Ferdinand and his wife were murdered here by a Serbian patriot on 28 June 1914, an action that dominoed most nations of Europe into the First World War. The Austrian repression after the assassinations was cruel, and many people were executed, some totally innocent.

Which bridge should I cross in Sarajevo for the road to Mostar and the Adriatic? One I tried was obviously wrong, so I followed George's commonsense method, got out of the car and showed the map to a man in shirtsleeves carrying a briefcase. He demonstrated that I ought not to bother with the river at all, but follow signposts for Illidze. 'The main road goes through it,' I took him to say, 'and when you get there you should have no more trouble.'

During the explanation he put two fingers to his temple, and gave the smile of a frog about to make a fatal leap into hot water, as if thinking me mad for not knowing what was so plain to him. Or he was trying to tell me that as an inhabitant of Sarajevo he intended blowing his brains out before nightfall. His continually moving lips, pulling another smile into shape, seemed to wish that I also might benefit the world by doing the same.

In such mountainous terrain the transport network was sparse, so it was easy to find the way south. The paved road, with many awkward bends, and at times perilous, took a westerly sweep so as to stay with the river and avoid the less inhabited areas.

Maize, tobacco, olives, grapes and figs grew around Jablanica, not always visible because of a gorge most of the way to Mostar, with peaks of 7,000 feet on both sides. Following the River Neretva, the road shadowed in places by darkening walls of cliff, it was easy to understand why such country had been used for guerrilla operations in the war, when Tito harried the Germans, and his partisans were harried in their turn.

Powerful cars, with an A for Austria sign plain at their rear ends, recklessly overtook. When one came up on the port bow, too close for my liking, indicators blinking to get around at any cost, I moved in as far as possible to give him leeway. He shot out on seeing an empty few hundred yards, but in the space a little motorised Yugo-box came from the other way frantically flashing headlights. Both vehicles seemed about to clash and disintegrate against the hillside, but the lucky Austrian got in by inches. I kept a good lookout from then on, for others pulling the same nightmarish stunt.

The minarets of Mostar appeared gracefully above the skyline, but after that place, as was plain from the map, the mountains fell away, and the road straightened at the delta of the Neretva. Near Buna two young men and a girl gave the hitchhiking signal, so I stopped, thinking I would be safer with passengers on board. An accident with only me in the car would mean one casualty, but I'd never risk injuring others, so from there on I would drive like a half-cut parson on his way to a parishioners' tea party. If the Austrians had unnerved me it was for the hitchhikers' benefit.

I learned from their fair English that they were students, wanting to go as far as Makarska some way up the coast. I asked how long they had been waiting. 'Almost an hour,' the girl said.

'What about all those Austrian cars? Wouldn't they have given you a lift?'

'We don't like such people.'

'They don't like us, either,' the girl laughed, as if well knowing reasons why not. 'In any case they're always in too much of a hurry to stop for anyone.'

They thought I was on holiday, and were amazed and amused on learning I had come from Russia. We stopped for coffee and snacks at a place they recommended on the coast. I had something to celebrate.

'*Thalassa!*' was the word that shot to mind and then the mouth, as one of Xenophon's vanguard turned to shout to his comrades after their long march, seeing the Ponte Euxine at Trebizon, on their way home from campaigning among the Persians in 401 BCE.

I had driven from the Baltic to the Adriatic and now, nearly 4,000 kilometres later, from the veranda of a café, I heard not the pebble grind of Dover Beach, or the grave lap of idle water on the Gulf of Finland, but the welcoming soft brush of an offshoot of the Mediterranean.

Childish to exult, while still mildly drunk as the different landscapes of the journey went through my mind. I stayed silent, my guests talking among themselves. The sight and sounds of the benign coastland told me that life was set fair to continue, that I had nothing to fear, but would remain the eternal outsider no matter how far I was tempted to appear compatible in the company of other people.

The rest of the afternoon took us to Makarska, where my agreeable passengers wanted to show me the town, and buy me a drink at one of the hotels. The place had been much bombed in the war, so was mostly modern. They told me that it had once been the dreaded hideout of pirates. It had also been the centre of the ancient heretical sect of the Bogomils, which denied – as I always had – the divine birth of Jesus, for which its members were persecuted as viciously in the East as were the Cathars in the West.

I intended reaching Split before dusk, so parted from my friends who seemed to have been with me much longer than a couple of hours. I would never see them again but, sociable and forthcoming, they would be long remembered.

Mountains sloped close to the road, but any attention that could be spared from the wheel was given to islands extending laterally from the mainland as if their shores were the walls of fjords, a panorama followed nearly the whole way to Italy.

In Split I arranged to stay two nights at a comfortable hotel. Fatigue, and the Palace of Diocletian detained me, a walled area laid out in the shape of a Roman castrum enclosing the Old Town (Stari Grad) and its population of several thousand. The ramparts, with towers at three of the corners, had been Diocletian's residence after his abdication in 305 BCE.

A stroll along the harbour front primed me for walking at dusk into its agglomeration of late antique architecture, the perfect time of the day to see it. I stood before the Temple of Jupiter and the mausoleum of the ex-Emperor. As far as I knew Piranesi had never used his pencil in those lugubrious streets without sun or light, but the heaviest of buildings reared massively up as if still waiting for him.

Tuesday, 24 July
I was drawn to the Old Town again, walking streets in the hot dry air, the buildings seeming somewhat less awesome in daylight. After lunch, pulled irresistibly back to the car, I drove sixty kilometres on unpaved roads to look at the town of Drnis, then wended a different route back on gravel surface to the coast at Trogir, a medieval town without the walls it had when an

important port under Venetian rule. The place of narrow streets was packed on an island joined to the mainland by a stone bridge. I walked to the cathedral where a sacristan claimed with glowing eyes that it was the most beautiful church in Dalmatia, and though I had as yet seen few others in that province I agreed that he must be right.

I drank half a bottle of wine on the outside terrace of the restaurant near the bridge, so had to keep a clear head going back to Split after supper. Nevertheless I couldn't turn down the offered slivovitz with my cigar. A gypsy woman and her daughter of about fourteen stood by the table, and on impulse I held out a hand for my fortune to be told.

The darkly costumed daughter, golden earrings dangling, stayed silent during the session, though her fixed Esmeralda smile more than made do for speech. But her eyes had no humour, showed a desperate sadness that had been there too long to cure or fathom, and I could only look at her now and again.

The mother – though they may not have been related – had lips and eyes that were far from gloomy, with the wit to understand immediately what was wanted. She took a pack of cards from her bag and laid several on the table I partially cleared. Perhaps by design she placed them at the farthest point so that I couldn't see clearly what they were, though I had no wish to know. The waiter looked disapprovingly but, seeing my interest, did not interfere.

She considered the display of gaudy pictures, which reminded me of those in childhood comic papers, and moved them about as if to fix the position of regiments before a battle. Taking one or two out of place, she thoughtfully shifted another, then glanced at the girl, and shook her head as if whatever had been divined was something I might not like to know.

I had always believed that 'the worst has already happened', not out of optimism that from then on all would be right, but because I didn't care one way or the other, an attitude good for work and therefore peace of mind. Such lackadaisical reasoning could have been a puerile attempt to divert the gods, yet might make whatever did come more interesting and therefore more possible to survive.

The girl nodded, as if giving her mother permission to speak, at which she stared into my eyes and said something I of course couldn't understand, a repeat of the words making no difference.

A burly Croat with a big moustache called from the next table: 'What she say, Englishman, is what is in your heart only God can know.' Then he laughed long and hard, perhaps thinking that I couldn't say what was there either.

I thanked him for an enlightenment which little surprised me, for it was true that I preferred to let whatever was there take care of itself. I gave the woman money to match the weight of her pronouncement, and watched the two of them crossing the causeway arm in arm back to the mainland, laughter reaching me till they were almost out of sight.

Wednesday, 5 July

Driving had become so much part of my existence as to seem there was no other, certainly none that I wanted. Filling sheets of paper at my desk was hardly thought about. I had left a book of stories half complete, and ideas for a couple of novels were somewhere in my head, but my body, confirmed by its position on the map, was that of the eternal motorised tramp going through land and seascapes only imaginable now that I was seeing them.

What did I think of while at the wheel? Did I think at all would be more realistic to ask. Not being a philosopher I did nothing except gather transitory impressions. Steering, changing gear and braking was instinctive and automatic.

I glanced as often as was safe at the scenery, also to muse, reflect, even recollect, knowing it was always possible that the next minute could be my last – a good way to live. Disordered thoughts came in tickertape fashion, and I could hardly remember what had gone through my consciousness the moment before. When the journey was over it would be no use wondering what I had been thinking at any one time, and however galling the lack turned out to be, the realisation that I might never be able to rewind that stream of rolling macadamised impressions was a fair price for such untroubled travelling.

At times I thought of George left behind in the Soviet Union, and his dream of one day visiting London. I regretted that, supposing he could find the money, he wasn't able to board a train for the Hook of Holland and take a ferry to Harwich. Or get on the first airliner out. Everything was wrong with a system that stopped him or anyone else going where they liked, which I'd always known. Why hadn't I said more than I had about it while in Moscow? Perhaps I should go back to Russia soon, and make my views even plainer, though what difference it would make who could say?

The road to Rijeka went between sheer hillsides and a nearby shoreline. Every risky moment on a curving rise showed rocky islands to the left, with bare rugged coasts. The bunched-up houses of a tiny medieval port or village usually had a ferry steaming outwards like a toy.

So absorbed, you might say contented, it wasn't till stopping to take a break for fuel and coffee that I saw I'd done 380 kilometres since Split. Beyond Rijeka I would pass no more islands, though having seen so many already there was little reason for regret. I had thought to put up at Rijeka, but it was early, and the vision of Italy, a mere fifty kilometres ahead, made it too tempting not to reach Venice before nightfall.

The road along the quayside at Rijeka was almost empty, a quiet place with few cars and people. Perhaps they were taking their siestas, as I should have been. The Austrian architecture was still there from the old days, though again like most ports in that region it had been much bombed in the war.

Before 1918 Fiume (as Rijeka was then called) was part of the Austro–Hungarian Empire, and a 'hotel' was put up opposite the rice mill, at the western end of the port, large enough to accommodate 3,000 people on their way to a better life in the United States. The 'huddled masses yearning to be free' came from all parts of central and southeastern Europe, and at the 'hotel' their health and papers were checked before being allowed on to the ships.

Fiume was held by the Croats in 1919, till the Italian novelist and poet, Gabriele d'Annunzio, led squads of freebooting ex-soldiers from Trieste and claimed the town for Italy. On his own responsibility he set up a fiefdom – the Regency of Carnaro – and as a poet and self-proclaimed governor entranced (or bored) the inhabitants with frequent dithyrambic speeches from the balcony of his town hall. He drew up a constitution, with a law for easy divorce, so that many Italians resolved their marital difficulties.

D'Annunzio had no support for his enterprise from the Italian government, which only wanted to get him out. The battleship *Andrea Doria* was ordered to bombard the place in 1920, and he came close to being killed, but he held the town in trust until it was finally allotted to Italy in 1924. Now it is back with Yugoslavia.

At the Italian frontier I swapped traveller's cheques for lire, and queued for my allowance of cheaper petrol coupons issued to tourists. A meal of meat and pasta, and a litre of water, set me up for more miles.

Bypassing Trieste, I thought of James Joyce and Italo Svevo, and also gave a nod to Duino where Rilke wrote his elegies. Locked on to the motorway, the local drivers hurled like rockets in their Fiats, Lamborghinis and Ferraris. My impulse was to put on speed but, still wary of the failed signalling system, I went at the usual rate, recalling the names of battles fought in that region against the Austrians in the First World War. Military history, from the time of Joshua, had always interested me, and now I crossed each sluggish river in its turn: the Isonzo, Tagliamento and Piave, on whose banks the Austrians were prevented from going on to Venice.

I left the motorway for the cul-de-sac of Lido di Iesolo, and after a while on the dead straight road I spotted a ramshackle hut on wasteland with a notice hanging from its side saying *Tutti Reparazione*, which I took to mean 'anything fixed'.

The area was littered with disembowelled vehicles, spare parts of every sort hooked on the outside walls, so I pulled in, to find out if anything could be done to repair the unserviceable blinkers which had bothered me all the way from Sweden.

A man by the door, wearing only shorts, was sprawled along the gravel, spannering bits into a motorbike. On my explaining by signs what was wrong, he said I was not to worry, came to the car, and put the bonnet up. He motioned me to sit on a stone for a few minutes, and went into his treasure store to search for the necessary spares.

I was halfway through a Partagas cigar by the time he had finished installing what I hoped were the correct fuses and bulbs. He asked me to test them, while he wiped dead midges from my windscreen with a damp rag. Switching them on, they worked. I had grown used to the anxiety, and now my worries were over. I felt too optimistic to imagine they might still, through the actions of a malign gremlin, fail to function in the next fifty miles.

The bill for work and parts was such a negligible amount that I gave him a Monte Cristo as well. The lights never failed again, and I was thanking him all the way to England whenever I had to overtake. Hurrah for Italian expertise!

The long tongue of land beyond the village of Iesolo led to the lido of that name, a resort area close to Venice. A friend who worked at the Hotel Ionio had arranged for me to stay there two nights.

After a shower and a nap I went with her to the end of the spit, from where the islands of Venice were visible, a couple of miles away. The sun on its decline spread a coppery glow over the towers and spires, my first view of the place. I recalled Shelley's lines, though he had written them at dawn:

> As within a furnace bright,
> Column, tower, and dome, and spire,
> Shine like obelisks of fire . . .

I was back in Western Europe, and nearer to home than God. My friend and I went to dinner at a good restaurant (I even put on a tie) to celebrate my safe arrival.

Thursday, 6 July

We caught the crowded morning boat, went weaving in a mist between islands to a mooring near the Piazza San Marco. It was only a reconnaissance, but a pleasure to walk. The square swarmed with pigeons and tourists, but a leisurely second breakfast inside a café cut off the sight of most. A twenty-minute glance in the cathedral told me I must look into my Ruskin later. A cardboard box could only hold so many maps and books.

After a few hours walking through streets and alleys the only sighs at the Bridge of Sighs concerned my feet. We had a late lunch at as ordinary a trattoria as could be found in such a tourist-ridden place. On deck in the afternoon, looking over the wake of the launch, the spires of Venice faded away.

Friday, 7 July

The last great barrier – the Alps – between me and the Channel loomed as I motorwayed the flat expanse of the Po lowlands, Dolomitic peaks sensed but not seen in skirting Vicenza and Verona, Brescia and Bergamo.

I felt no hurry on swinging north from Monza towards Como, merely going at the by now accustomed pace, recalling yesterday's marvels in Venice, and almost missed the bifurcation for the Swiss border. Had I done so – that impulsive and treacherous left turn again – I would have been shunted to the Simplon Pass and out of Switzerland by Lausanne, not on my planned route. A one-second swerve at the vital split of the motorway spun me in the right direction, and it was lucky that no other traffic was close enough to be disturbed by the abrupt manoeuvre.

The unmistakable mass drew close, under a moil of grey

cloud about to send rain on to all cars as they went through the frontier post at Chiasso. I knew that even in July there could be snow on the St Gotthard where I was heading.

After the formalities I changed the remaining lire into francs, and bought a couple of Swiss maps at the 1:200,000 scale which showed the route as far as Basel. Two youths signalled they were hitchhiking, so I stopped for them. Twenty years old and on their way home to Holland, they said they would be grateful for a lift as far as the Rhine, 300 kilometres in a northerly direction.

They laid their rucksacks in the back and came on board. 'It's Friday,' I said, 'your lucky day,' and off we went, up and over wooded foothills to the glistening Lake of Lugano. Negotiating a range by an 1,800-foot pass, imposing scenery was again in my theatre, until we were on a straight road to Bellinzona by the River Ticino, My passengers said they had been south to Sicily, and had done well in getting lifts from kindly Italians.

The valley gave a gradual ascent as far as Airollo, when the hard work began, a thousand-metre climb in a few miles by thirty-eight well-laid hairpin bends, which one of the Dutchmen began carefully to count. I told him soon enough amid much laughter that if he clocked another bloody curve I'd stop the car and throw him into the foaming torrent.

The pass was a dreary open space, with scattered small lakes between sombre mountain walls. At 7,000 feet we were in a different climatic zone, snow in patches looking like dull milk, the scene bleak in its dearth of any comforting vegetation. Walking towards the gaunt hotel for coffee, the air felt bitterly cold after so long a time driving in the heat, and I looked hopefully for a renowned woolly-bully of a St Gotthard Newfoundland dog with a barrel of brandy swinging from its neck.

The road to Andermatt and Altdorf, through icy drizzle for a while, gave way to tantalising views of tortuous cliffs around the Vierwald Statter See, specks which must have been boats on flashes of sheet metal. I wondered whether to pull in and spend the night at one of the comfortable hostelries passed now and again, lights glowing in their windows. Instead we took a long time circuiting the in and out configuration of the three lakes, and it was nearly dusk when driving through Lucerne.

As usual darkness caught up with me, and I found it difficult to stop. Should I maintain a compass course pointing to Basel and follow it through the night? My passengers were relaxed enough not to care, though I assumed that the sooner we reached the Rhine before calling it a day the better.

Exhaustion, however, was gritting up my eyes and, not wanting to endanger any of us, I thought Olten would be a convenient place to bed down, yet the inside demon hastened me through. Again on the open road I had to admit that, after 400 miles, enough was enough, and I disliked driving in darkness, so a lodging of some sort had to be found.

The road took a hairpin turn to the west for about a mile, then by a similar sharp bend went back east, straightening out at the village of Hauenstein. Under a street light I saw a large unlit building with a sign in the window: *Zimmer*, meaning of course that there were rooms to let.

It was ten o'clock, and the street was empty. The house was without lights and shuttered up, but I thumped the door till a man who looked like a farmer came from around the back, asked what so much noise was about, and what I wanted. It seemed obvious to me, but I told him in pidgin German that the three of us needed a room for the night. When he smiled and said he had one for us I called to the lads who were dozing in the car. He showed us into a large room with four single beds. I paid the tariff for all three in advance so that we could set off early in the morning. On asking about a place for supper he thought I was daft, because all possibilities were closed at such an hour.

Leftover sandwiches – the cornucopia package made up at the hotel in Iesolo – provided us with sufficient fodder to sleep afterwards. We sat on the beds too tired to do more than munch in the dim light.

Saturday, 8 July

The room was hardly quiet, from so much passing traffic, but it was agreed on waking at half past seven that we had slept like moss-covered stones. Yawns were contagious while packing our few things, but lessened after a plentiful Swiss breakfast.

An early drizzle on going through the Jura hills soon fulfilled its prophecy of good weather. Steering between trams and lorries in Basel, I let the youths off at a safe place so that they could try their luck on the German motorways to Holland. Wishing them Godspeed, they asked for my address and, being well brought up, promised to send a thank-you letter on getting home – which they did.

In France I set the nose of the veteran Peugeot on to the open roads of its homeland, but it went leisurely at first, as if to sniff the full sweetness of the soil. I bought fresh supplies of food in Altkirch, then sent a telegram from the post office thanking the manager of the Hotel Ionio for his generosity in having let me stay two nights free. I later posted a parcel of signed books.

The car pulled me through *le trou de Belfort*, that topographical feature so tempting to an invading army. After Vesoul and Langres I gave an almost mute soldier a lift from

Chaumont to Troyes, then pushed on to Château Thierry, Soissons and Ham.

I called at Coucy-le-Château Auffrique hoping to find a bed, but it was Saturday and the hotel was full. I strolled around the village wanting a look at the castle, or what was left of it. It had once been a remarkable example of medieval military architecture, but in 1918 the Germans blew it up in their retreat, even though it had no tactical significance. Heaps of debris remained after such 'wanton and destructive vandalism', as the 1920 Blue Guide to *Belgium and the Western Front* informed me.

Trundling into Bapaume, six hundred kilometres from Hauenstein, I was back in the north, and could have been over the Channel well before midnight, and home by early morning, but I had no will to charge on. Like an aircraft in an emergency landing searching for a place to set down without alarming its passengers, I didn't want to frighten the devils still in me by a too abrupt end to the journey.

At dusk a ribbed cloud filled the sky like the skeleton of a giant predatory bird, and I recalled reading *From Bapaume to Paschendaele* by the journalist Philip Gibbs when I was twenty, a narrative of battles in the Great War, which began my obsession with the history of that dire four years.

I pulled up at the Hôtel de la Paix on the main street, a convenient place to stay, but was satisfied with a meal and glass of wine, intending to sleep in the car. With the help of a Michelin map bought at the last filling station I went south of Bapaume and parked at a British military cemetery, half a kilometre from the nearest village.

Darkness and isolation was soothing after the drive, and though it was early I lowered the front seat to make a more or less level bed, and stretched out under a blanket. I slept awhile, but woke because an unexplained regular sharp click sounded every minute or so of the chilly night from behind the dashboard. I thought the disturbance came from the clock, then couldn't be sure. Proper rest was impossible, and the loud singing of birds soon signified that daybreak was close.

I came out of a coma rather than proper slumber, also because the spot I had parked at wasn't as isolated as I had hoped it would be, since huge lorries going to Lille or Paris on the motorway were audible for much of the time. Silence makes even the slightest noise loud.

Sunday, 9 July
Stirring, I took a gulp of brandy and ate bread and cheese. A faint light glowed in the east and, unable to be still, I drove at half past three along the empty road to Bapaume. Turning southwest to Flers and Longueval, fields and hedges were sharp enough etched for the car lights to be switched off. No good farmer was awake, shutters still closed at the houses. Mist lay in the hollows but land above rolled openly against the sky, a dark patch of wood looming here and there. Humps and hollows of greensward on the edge of Delville Wood (Devils Wood to the soldiers) told even now where fighting had taken place half a century before.

The sky was leaden and birds noisy as I drove slowly out of Longueval to High Wood, a flank of packed trees formidable even now in the dawn.

The British took it on 14 July 1916, when it was almost empty of Germans, but several hours elapsed before reinforcements could be brought up, and so it was recaptured. British battalions spent weeks in attack and counterattack, and it was only occupied after two months of fighting. In one assault Robert Graves's lungs were riddled with shrapnel, and he was reported killed in action on his twenty-first birthday – though he lived to be ninety.

I wanted to explore the wood, but a piece of board informed the public that trespassers would be prosecuted. I went along the field to look for a gap but it was so firmly fenced that, as in the Great War, the heaviest wirecutters would have been necessary to make a breach.

In London I had recently come across a cloth-mounted War Office Trench Map in a secondhand bookshop, for a shilling. The scale was about six inches to the mile, and it covered the Gommecourt sector of the front where, on 1 July 1916, two battalions of Sherwood Foresters had been annihilated by German artillery and machine-gun fire while trying to cross no-man's-land on the first day of the Somme Offensive. An uncle of mine had been taken prisoner, and I wanted to see the scene of the disaster.

On the way to Gommecourt I glanced now and again at the outspread map on the passenger seat, showing the German defences, one line behind the other running from southwest to northeast in red. The British front was indicated by a dotted line in blue, a mere five hundred yards separating the different colouring.

I reconnoitred the ground, as if to find the spot where my uncle had laid before he was captured. The silent fields were now planted with corn, potatoes and barley, but when the Foresters went 'over the top' – suicidally laden with seventy pounds of equipment, after a week of bombardment, heavy work shoring up their trenches, lack of sleep, little food, and soaked from mud and rain – they had no chance.

Examining the area between the trenches through binoculars, it was no longer pitted with craters, but a wide gently sloping meadow of rich grass. With bread and ham bought in a shop in Fonquevillers I sat on the cemetery wall of Gommecourt Wood by the laneside trying to imagine the emotions of the men as they climbed out of their trenches at seven o'clock and advanced into a storm of shells and machine-gun fire.

Rows of well-tended graves behind me were each marked with a cross, many nameless headstones having: 'Known only unto God' chiselled into the concrete. I took notes for a possible novel, or family memoir, about my young soldier uncle and his mates caught in the kind of warfare they'd had no conception of when so blithely enlisting. Perhaps the theme would tell how the conflict, triggered by those fatal shots in Sarajevo, affected not only them but their families as well. I would call the book *Raw Material*.

I drove to the valley of the Ancre, and made my way, by a little bending of the fence, into Aveluy Wood. The trees had grown again, though not to any great height, yet made enough shelter to hide a trespasser by also keeping out much of the light.

The mulch-covered ground was indented where craters had been, and there were no recognisable paths through the greenery, though many were marked on the map. Banks of earth along shallow yet distinct trenches revealed bits of rusty wire and iron spikes, pieces of shovel and decaying metal of all sorts scattered under the leaves. Perhaps deeper down there were bones, because 4,000 Yorkshiremen had formed up there, many killed and wounded before emerging to attack Thiepval. I could only suppose that if I had been eighteen at the time I would have enlisted with everyone else.

I considered taking a marlin spike as a souvenir, but threw it down. Quantities of live shells, grenades and small arms ammunition were still collected every year, unearthed by farmers while ploughing. Woods were also dangerous, and people hunting for mementoes were sometimes killed or maimed.

My feet were trapped in the undergrowth, legs buckling at a hidden trench or the ridge of a shell hole. Ghosts lurked everywhere, though I laughed at the notion on pulling myself free. Tramping feet and the crack of dead twigs broke the silence again, and spiders wove their dewy gossamers, but it was eerie being alone in such a place.

Losing all sense of direction, I wondered how I would find a way to the car. A lack of orientation was no longer amusing. I stopped to light a cigar found in my pocket. In a clearing a line on the sun showed the direction for getting back to the solid ground of a paved lane, and I was glad to be away from trees that had fed on so much blood they seemed almost animal.

Back at the Hôtel de la Paix in Bapaume I booked a room for the night – the last one. On going in to supper I heard a tall blowsy red-haired Englishwoman (undeniably attractive) being told there wasn't a bed left. She seemed about to stamp her foot at the disappointment, but the proprietor helpfully telephoned a hotel in Albert, where she would be able to stay.

I had wondered whether to give up my room, as a gentleman ought, and sleep in the car again. Or I could offer to stretch out on the floor while she had the bed, and who knew what would come of that? But it was light enough for her to reach Albert less than twenty kilometres down the straight road, so I merely recorded the incident in the same notebook for a story sometime.

Monday, 10 July

Military cemeteries, and battlefields from which they were made, lay thickly about northwest France and a slice of Belgium. Still feeling no urgent reason to hurry across the Channel I headed north for Ypres via Arras, Lens and Armentières, through landscapes of peace, husbandry and life, over one stretch of open land after another.

A brasserie off the main square at Ypres was thick with the odours of roast meat, rather better chips than could usually be found in England, salad dressing, coffee and tobacco, all of which successfully tempted me into ordering a bigger lunch than could be taken in.

I walked to the Menin Gate, the entrance into the 'Immortal Salient', where tens of thousands had gone and not come back. The memorial complex, opened in 1927, and designed by Sir Reginald Blomfield, looked like a great Pharoanic temple from the outside.

Above the main archway was a couchant lion, sombre though handsome, carved by Reid Dick. On the walls inside, and the steps and galleries leading to the Vauban ramparts, were chiselled the names of 55,000 who had been killed in the Salient but had no known graves.

I recalled the walls of the Old Synagogue in Prague on which, similarly inscribed, were the names of 77,000 Czech Jews taken away by the Germans and murdered, women and children among them. A greater chill came from comparing the difference in numbers.

A drive northeast on a slightly ascending road took me by the Tyne Cot Cemetery (12,000 graves) to the village of Paschendaele 130 feet above sea level. Its heap of ruins was taken with heavy loss by the Canadians, and ended the Third

Battle of Ypres on 6 November 1917. The offensive had opened three months before, but persistent rain created a beleaguered region of mud in which overladen soldiers and wounded often drowned. Fighting in it was as the Official History said 'the last word in human misery . . . in conditions hitherto unknown in war'. The soldiers endured and fought on. Out of five million who took part in the battles a million came back wounded, and three hundred thousand were killed.

Dry and cultivated land sloped down to Ypres in the distance, farms and houses resurrected after the wilderness of fifty years ago. To the east Paschendaele overlooked the glistening plain of Flanders, which the soldiers had been striving to reach but didn't until the final breakthrough in 1918.

I closed my notebook, having seen enough, and drove to Malo-les-Bains, back in France, where I booked into a modest pension for the night. Would men in white coats have to drag me kicking and expostulating home? How long before I admitted that my time was up, and voted with my feet to go like a responsible person? I walked back and forth along the beach, with a westerly glance towards Dover, which I couldn't see, reluctant to give up the false joy of having no roots anywhere, and break the calm achieved in the last month.

Yet I must get back to work, having notions and material for much. In books it was easier to make others live for me, whether they wanted to or not. I would golemise to my advantage, until meeting someone from my pen I recognised as myself. Then I would stop, though it was an event hard to imagine.

I was nothing if not a writer, and travelling had to lose its power. Better to go sooner rather than later.

Dinner at the pension, a bottle of Bordeaux to hand, began with soup, then pâté de campagne, with toast, butter, and thinly sliced gherkins, followed by a main course of chicken, and then the inevitable feathery light crème caramel. Cointreau after the coffee called for a cigar, whose stub (it was a forty, George) sizzled into the water as I watched ships entering and coming out of nearby Dunkirk.

Tuesday, 11 July

It was an almost-nothing stage to Calais, hardly noticed in the pull of home, intentions that had been so subdued now automatically in motion. On the boat by midday, I first of all called at the wireless cabin to write a telegram telling of my arrival in London, even if only to stand outside the radio office window, opened due to the heat, and check the perfectly transmitted words of my message on their way in Morse, which told me more than anything that there was no turning back. I was not even certain it would arrive in time.

Halfway across the water, standing on the topmost deck – so far from Russia – I looked forward to the future with interest and curiosity, no matter what the gypsy woman had said in Trogir. Revivified in the month since leaving Harwich, I had become another person, hardly as yet imaginable to myself, but on getting to England I must meet the old me to a certain extent, and become him again as far as I could. I was at heart a wanderer, but such a life could not go on for ever, and though I had often asked why not, 8,000 kilometres in the car had surely to be enough.

From Dover I redrilled myself into hugging the left-hand lane, but since it was the natural side of the road for the car it was easy enough to go with the traffic, grateful for the bit of motorway between Faversham and Chatham.

In little more than a couple of hours re-entry into the home atmosphere was cushioned on finding Ted Hughes and Assia Wevill (Guttman) in the house, where they'd had lunch. They watched with much laughter as I unloaded my Russian loot, which included, among much else, balalaikas, metal holders for glasses of tea, and art books. A bottle of vodka and a jar of caviar were soon unsealed, and we set to while David sat on the floor with his toys.

Part Two

Gadfly
1967

Friday, 1 September

The four-engined Tupolev was some way from touchdown, but my popping eardrums suggested we were slowly descending. A flashing light on the horizon – as I looked up from another reading of *Moby Dick* – turned out to be a navigation indicator.

A couple of months after the motoring trip I was going back to Moscow, with plane tickets and accommodation vouchers prepaid in hard currency. The visa classed me as a tourist, so I could not expect favours from the Writers' Union. The treasury in London allowed me to take out the limit of fifty pounds in traveller's cheques – a mean amount – but a few fivers smuggled in a back pocket were there to take care of any overspending.

On previous visits I'd said little of what had been in my mind about the political situation, but this time, because of my independent status, I could come out with what I liked. Friends, such as George Andjaparidze, my companion of the summer drive, would I felt sure remain staunch.

The track of the crowded aircraft followed the radio beam, until a grating under the fuselage, and the placid unwinking lights of rural Russia, told me we were close to landing.

Oksana met me at the terminal – out of courtesy I had told only her of my visit – her friendly face as if to keep me from feeling bored or beleaguered during my stay, though I had no worries about that.

After dinner in the hotel I went to the foreign currency bar, and met a group of men from Finland who were in Moscow to see a textile exhibition. One told me how happy he was that trade between England and his country was in such a thriving state. He was impressed by my recent automobile travels, and another Finn, curious to know whether I'd had any problems, said he wouldn't imagine so because English cars, being the best in the world, were made for the rough roads in Russia. I thought he must be joking, in his tall deadpan way, though he seemed not to be.

My first car had been English, I said, and while still brand new, during a trip to Morocco, the clutch went. When I wrote to the manufacturers, hoping to claim compensation on the guarantee due to careless workmanship in the factory, they huffily replied that whatever had gone wrong had been my fault and not theirs. It was up to me to have the matter put right – which I did.

Going on with my story to the surprised Finn, I told how, while driving out of Tangier one day after heavy rain, the same car stalled in a sheet of water from an overflowing stream. A Frenchman, seeing my plight, locked the front bumper of his sturdy Peugeot 403 on to my vehicle and pushed it all the way up the winding road to where I lived. I offered him a drink in the house but he called with a friendly wave that he hadn't time, though I'd taken him well out of his way. In England a couple of years later I bought the reliable Peugeot 404 that had taken me through Russia that summer.

Talk spun on to other topics, and one of the Finns said that spending the night with a lovely Russian girl cost only ten pounds. After a second vodka – he and his friends were drinking the finest malt whisky – I left them chatting to two young beauties who came into the room like queens.

In Moscow's top-class hotels the oldest trade is a way of extracting hard currency from foreign pockets, and the women also seemed to be enjoying their status at the bar. I thought good luck to them, because it was all part of the black economy that kept the Soviet system running.

At midnight I lay in bed listening to a melancholy performance of the Kinks on my tape recorder, relishing a further period of mindlessness in Moscow. How far out could one get? Further than that, I hoped, at the sound of giant street-washing vehicles growling by outside. Moscow must be the cleanest city in the world, washed, shampooed and set every night.

Saturday, 2 September
Breakfast came punctually to my room, avoiding half an hour's wait in the restaurant. The first swig of lemon tea seemed to improve my eyesight, as if I had put on glasses.

I met George at ten by the Gorki Street post office. After the embrace and backslapping we lit up cigars and talked all the way to Red Square, recalling the highlights of our motor trip. He asked about the latest interesting novels in London, and all I could do was mention again *Smallcreep's Day* by Peter Currell Brown, a sort of Kafkalike incursion into the anonymous world of a vast factory.

We lunched at the Writers' Union, where Oksana joined us. George enthused about Gagra on the Black Sea, how delightfully sub-tropical it was, summer the whole year round, and full of lovely girls. 'It's far better than your Riviera on the Mediterranean,' he said to me. 'When it gets too warm you can go for a walk in the mountains. It's the most beautiful spot, even better than the Crimea.'

'Let's go, then,' I said. 'I'll see whether you're right or not. A few days there would fit me up nicely. How much do the air tickets cost? We could go today.'

'Not much. About 400 roubles.' He knew that my *luftmensch* mind had no intention of clicking out of zero and and lighting off, but Oksana, as if to discourage me from doing so, asked what I had done after she had seen me to my hotel the previous evening.

Wanting to shake her Soviet complacency I told her that after supper I had gone into the foreign currency bar, but instead of paying ten pounds and waltzing off with a beautiful woman for the night, I decided to go for a walk, needing some exercise after more than three hours in the plane. 'There weren't many people in the streets by then, so it was pleasant. Turning off the boulevard I came to a block of flats that looked a bit run down, but out of curiosity I wandered into the courtyard, and saw a dim bulb over a doorway, where steps led down into a basement.

'At the bottom I, pushed my way through a curtain made of what looked like sackcloth, and saw half a dozen men and a couple of women around a table, playing cards for money. It was like a scene out of Dostoevsky, but they were all quite jolly, and invited me to sit down. I needed no second telling, and in spite of my monkey Russian I managed to get through a couple of games. I seemed to amuse them very much, and one of the laughing women – a perfect Grushenka with exquisite grey Kirghiz eyes – poured me a glass of vodka. I was getting in touch with the real Russia at last. A man with a scar on his cheek, in an oilskin jacket even though the place was warm, said he was a train driver who made a lot of money smuggling people across the frontier – though he may have been joking. He gave me a piece of bread and some salty herring, and filled my glass again.

I'd got my tape recorder with me, so switched it on and played them the Kinks, which they loved, and tried to dance to.

'I lost a few roubles at cards, but when I offered to settle the debt with a couple of five-pound notes they took them gladly. The women loved the picture of Queen Elizabeth. After a couple of hours – it must have been midnight – I shook hands with them all and left. I pushed the curtain aside and walked back to the street. Half cut by then, I was just able to find my way back to the hotel.'

What I had intended to be an amusing anecdote for Oksana's benefit put a look of alarm and disapproval on her face. She was convinced that all I had said was true. She was flushed and fearful: 'There are such people in the city, or so I've heard, but you shouldn't have gone there. It's very dangerous to mix with types like that. You were lucky not to have been robbed. The police catch them sometimes, and send them away from Moscow.'

I regretted the tale, but hadn't thought she'd believe it, while George was more familiar with my spiralling imagination. 'It sounds a real cock-and-bull story to me.'

I admitted that it was, though could never be sure Oksana finally believed me.

In the evening we taxied to a party at Valentina Ivasheva's. The vestibule of the block of flats was gloomy, a low wattage bulb showing broken bottles and a few tins underfoot. When I mentioned this to Valentina on getting upstairs she said anxiously: 'Hurry inside. I know all about that. Hooligans come from the next block and throw bottles in the entrance. They don't like us because we're only writers and journalists in this building.'

I was amused. 'But if the housing authorities mixed everyone up a bit more you'd get to know each other and become friendly. Then it might not happen,' I suggested.

'Oh no,' she said, 'we wouldn't want that sort of person in here.'

Talk at the party was mostly about Ilya Ehrenberg, who had died and was to be buried on Monday. After telling Oksana I'd read his masterpiece *The Fall of Paris*, and very much admired other works of his, she promised to wangle a permit from the Writers' Union, so that we could go to the funeral.

On the boulevard at past midnight it seemed we'd never get a taxi. Even those showing vacancy lights went by as if with wings and about to achieve lift off. Whether set for home after the day's work, or on call to special customers, I didn't know, but damned them nevertheless, George solved the problem, by muttering into my ear: 'Hold some foreign money up, and see what happens.'

Rain was falling so heavily that few people were on the streets. Oksana said it was typical Moscow weather for the time of year. I took a few pound notes from my wallet, stepped into the road, and wiggled them high. Within minutes a car skidded to a stop. The cash was taken, we climbed in, and off we went, enough currency for the driver to deliver George and Oksana to their homes, and me to the hotel.

From the window of my room I watched streaks of blue lightning tearing holes in the paperbag sky. Thunder rolled around the squares and boulevards as if Kremlin guns were celebrating another town taken from the Germans.

Sunday, 3 September

A pleasant time touring the town with Oksana's daughter, who has the good looks of a Persian princess. We picnicked by the banks of the river, talking of many things.

Monday, 4 September

Grey street-cleaning wagons parked nose to tail, not an inch between, barricaded the road so that those going into the Writers' Union to pay their respects would not be disturbed. Inside, ushers with black armbands slashed with red pointed me to the visitors' book so that I could leave my simple message of condolence before following the file into the main hall where the dead writer lay. Tchaikovsky's 'Pathétique' played through loudspeakers.

Ehrenberg was receiving honours that might have been more muted had Stalin been alive. He was born in 1891, into an assimilated middle-class Jewish family in Kiev. Because of his youthful revolutionary activities he had to leave Russia, and lived in Paris until the Bolshevik *coup d'état* in 1917. Four years later he left again, and only went back when the Germans invaded the Soviet Union in 1941. During the war – the Great Patriotic War – he put his journalistic skills into encouraging hatred of Nazi Germany.

His articles made him popular with the soldiers of the Red Army, and later kept him safe from Stalin. Always a writer of independent views, his novel *A Prayer for Russia* (1921) described the miseries of Bolshevik rule, while *Julio Jurenito* (1922) dealt with the dislike of intellectuals in both capitalist society and over disciplined communism.

His loyalty to the Soviet regime was always conditional. *People and Life*, his last book, gave a true account of the opinions of Russian and Western writers during the 1920s and 1930s. He had always done his best to steer a humane course through dangerous times, and was in the vanguard of liberalisation after Stalin's death in 1952. So it was obvious that none of the crowd endeavouring to pay their respects held it against him for managing to stay out of the tyrant's clutches.

The face in the coffin, surrounded by flowers as white as snow, didn't appear fully dead, as if he might impetuously sit up and wonder what was going on. Some who looked at his corpse seemed in a state of shock, as if not knowing what would happen in society now that he was dead, their sideways expressions followed by a glance at the huge framed photograph suspended above – before they drifted on.

Officials from Czechoslovakia said their tributes, then Montague, the delegate from Great Britain, gave a short speech. I had been asked to, but preferred to be an anonymous mourner. A man from France commented on Ehrenberg's years in Paris, and mentioned the prejudice he had always faced because of being Jewish.

At the Novodyevichi Cemetery Oksana realised she had forgotten our passes for the graveside ceremony. Not wanting her to be upset at the mistake I told her it would be far more interesting to stay with the crowd held at barriers across the road by the entrance. Lorries of standing people cruised by, the sides crêped with red and black banners, while all the windows of neighbouring flats had their silent spectators.

Young soldiers linked arms to prevent a rush for the gate, until shouts from the crowd deepened in tone, as if they could be angry now that the rain had stopped. With their wreaths and flowers they were tired of being kept in place, and determined to show their will this time. A sudden unrehearsed surge took them forward, and the line was broken. They ran across the space and scuffled with the militia as the coffin was going through, and I was pleased that scores made their way in behind.

Tuesday, 5 Septenber
After talking to people from Intourist about how much I was enjoying my holiday in the USSR, George took me to a showing of Bondarchuk's *War and Peace*. I had been interested in his work since seeing *The Fate of a Man*, based on a story by Sholokhov, which I came across in a Tangier cinema. Though subtitled and hardly a good print it was obviously a great film. A Red Army soldier is knocked out in battle, and before he can recover his senses and flee he is taken prisoner by the Germans. After the war many such returning men were packed off to camps in Siberia, though this soldier escapes at least that fate. Bondarchuk's handling of someone who was regarded almost as a traitor for having, apparently, surrendered to the enemy, was humane and understanding.

Back in Russia the soldier wanders about the country trying to make sense of what has happened to him. There's a hint of some kind of future when he befriends an obviously abandoned child found pottering around in the squalor. He extends a hand to the orphan – no words necessary – and takes him away, presumably to bring him up.

The film wasn't much liked by the authorities, though it had after all been made. Some didn't agree with my unqualified praise when talking about it, and I did not know enough Russian to ask an ordinary man in the street what he thought of it, but felt sure he would have been sympathetic to the soldier's plight.

Wednesday, 6 September

A young woman from Intourist, Irena, who was to be my companion and guide, took me to an office where we booked seats on the train for Vladimir, 200 kilometres to the east. After nearly a week in Moscow I was glad to spend a couple of days somewhere else.

The carriage was comfortable, with seating of similar style to those in an aircraft, though more spacious, and the electrified line gave a smooth ride. Shortly after departure, when a man leaned across the gangway and enquired if I was an Estonian, I recalled the old woman in Novgorod who had asked the same. This time also I had to say no.

When pressed as to why the man thought so he merely said I looked like one, and went back to his newspaper. Could it be there was Estonian blood in me from way back? Perhaps some ancestral member of a Baltic Brotherhood had in olden days been shipwrecked at the mouth of the Humber and, losing his bearings from anguish and homesickness had, instead of making northeast, staggered along the banks of the Trent to Nottingham. If so, the thinning blood of his berserker spirit must have been much watered down by intermarrying with the civilised English – though it wasn't a likely story.

Telling Irena about my motor travels in the summer she was preternaturally interested in the crossing of Transylvania, because of its association with vampires. What did I know about them?

'Nothing. I never met one. I was wearing a bulb of garlic around my neck, so they left me alone!'

'Vampirism is a perversion,' she informed me, and I wondered whether she was referring to the sexual proclivities of the bat itself, or using the word to indicate a psychological or psychopathic condition. If the latter, perhaps the reason people became vampirish had to do with the deprivation of milk at the mother's breast during the first months of life.

It was hard to know how I'd picked up such assumptions, but I went on to say that some children are emotionally under-developed, and unable to become normal on growing up, for quite mysterious reasons, which results in them taking on the protection of a 'vampire complex'. On the other hand it could be that those who show serious symptoms of underdevelopment one day, and alarming maturity the next (for I suppose there must be such people) turn into writers and artists.

This supposition brought a strange expression on to her pale and rounded face, but what more could I think of to amuse or horrify her – and pass the time? On more solid ground I told her about the 1930s film with Bela Lugosi, *Vampire Bat* which I'd seen at eleven.

'As a child?' she exclaimed. 'How could someone so young be permitted to see it?'

'We just lied to the doorman that we were fourteen, and held out our money.' I then set her cheeks aglow by relating the plot of *Carmilla* by Sheridan Le Fanu, which may have been treading on very unSoviet ground, though I couldn't be sure, because the topic kept us talking to the end of our journey.

There were many churches and monasteries in Vladimir, most with views of the surrounding plain. The Gothic and baroque ecclesiastical monuments of Spain had usually brought on a feeling of wariness and even dread, but in Russia the graceful curves and domes of grandiose buildings calmed and enchanted. In gold, blue, white and green, they were invariably set in spectacular situations, and the holy Russian architecture of Vladimir matched if it did not exceed that of Kiev, Novgorod and Zagorsk.

Clusters of evening lights on the plain were like islands on a dark sea. Though train whistles and the hooters of shunting diesels sounded all night, and a noisy open-air dancing place close to one of the nearby cathedrals pumped away, I nevertheless slept long and well, agreeably woken by the cloth-footed musical bells of Old Russia.

Thursday, 7 September

Behind a cluster of church domes bushes of grey smoke from a factory chimney flattened along the underbelly of the sky. Vladimir was also an industrial city.

On the chilly morning below slowly whitening clouds we went forty kilometres by Intourist car to Suzdal. The Cathedral of the Nativity inside the Kremlin walls was built in 1528, but not being a student of churches I walked by the wonders quickly, a glance at icons and other details in passing, and hoping something would stay in the mind. It rarely did. I wanted vistas rather than close-up work.

Outside the Pokrovsky Convent a bow-legged black cockerel strutted like a formidable bulldog, so fiercely jealous of its territory that even a cat ran away in terror. We explored churches and monasteries at Bogolyubovo and Pokrov-on-the-Neri, till my eyes were almost blinded by the dazzle of so many icons.

The past closed itself off, so that all senses could as firmly as possible take in the present. I relished not feeling any responsibility for either past or present, for myself or others. On mentioning the mood to Irena she declared that it was against life to be that way. It was self-indulgence, she said, and would have to be atoned for when back in the real world. 'Maybe you're right,' I admitted, though dazzled more and more by such aesthetic products of the art of painting, but knowing that if I did have to pay for how I felt at the moment it would be by writing, in which the novelty of invented people would be my judges and hear me out.

With so many masterpieces of Byzantine architecture it became impossible to separate one church from another, in spite of taking notes, and I didn't seem capable of wielding a camera any more. From the main highway we followed a lane between wooden houses, and went under a railway bridge to a gently humped pasture where a few dozen cows grazed. Tracks multiplied, so we drove over open fields towards a small white church standing before a line of dark woods.

We left the car by a copse of birch trees, and from the opposite side of a broad lake the entire reflection of a white church shimmered in the water. Nearby, behind another church, a one-storey building had been divided into apartments. 'For architectural students to stay in the summer,' Irena said.

An elderly kerchiefed woman looking after a boy playing with a large ginger cat (its ears seriously lopsided) was the caretaker. Cats have as much personality as people, and who can say why, unless it's the way they look at us, or as we perceive them. The boy turned the animal this way and that in his arms, and the cat, endeavouring to settle on the direction it was required to look, while disconcerted by an anxiety it could well have done without, was only waiting for a lack of alertness on the boy's part to leap away to the woods, till hunger struck and it had to come home.

Friday, 8 September

On the 07.50 train back to Moscow I made up a story for Irena, which was what she may have expected from a writer, of two foreign couples who planned a joint visit to Vladimir. At the last moment the wife of one man didn't feel like leaving Moscow, and the husband of the other couple also decided to stay behind. Thus the pair who went became familiar with each other on the train, an intimacy that intensified in their romantic strolls from one church to another. 'What about the couple left behind?' Irena asked. 'Did something similar happen to them?'

'Not much. That's the main part of the story, though I suppose something could be made to happen.' She finally thought the plot too mechanical, and so did I, though most plots have to be, I said, which is why I can't always be bothered with them, certainly not the most obvious ones. 'I shan't write it, in any case.'

Taking the Metro, I was soon back at the hotel. In my room the telephone rang, and an interview was set up. A few minutes later it sounded again, and I was asked to do another. Magazines and publishers wanted to see me. Should I be flattered, or tell them to get lost? Unable to decide one way or the other, but knowing it was unrealistic to imagine I could come to Russia and not be asked to do such chores, I agreed to what was possible in the time available. To spend the days alone was much desired, but what would I have done beyond some unprofitable walking? So I decided to accept whatever was wanted with as good a grace as could be mustered.

On being wakened from an afternoon sleep, by a photographer requesting pictures of me in Red Square for the *Moscow News,* I went out to meet her.

She was young, with a perfectly shaped pretty face in that

doll-like pink cheeked Russian way, and tried her charms on a well-scarfed grandmother and her two charges into cosily posing by my side. Was I to pick the kids up and give them a kiss? Or splodge one on the old woman? The children were well enough dressed to belong to a wealthy official family, and looked at me as dourly as did the woman, who said something to the girl which I imagined to be the Russian equivalent of fuck off.

I didn't blame her, and drew the line at the experiment anyway, but the girl wasn't discouraged, and suggested a shot of me eating an ice cream. I told her I wasn't hungry, and that I would only be photographed without such accompaniments, recalling a cameraman from a London newspaper who, asking me to ride into an Arab market in Tangier on a donkey, got an abusive refusal.

I was more annoyed with my nonco-operation than at the girl's request, so kept my sense of humour and, not wanting her to get into trouble with her editor, knowing she had a living to make, and was ambitious (though I didn't see what she would get out of her appointment with me) I agreed to have photographs taken against the background of Lenin's tomb.

I was later telephoned by someone from *Novy Mir* magazine asking if I would give a lecture on modern writing at the university-style Gorki Institute of Literature, a prestigious training ground for young Soviet writers. That sort of thing was what I had been waiting for, and though I was by now somewhat fed up with so many requests, I tried not to sound too abrupt on agreeing to do it.

So instead of walking the streets as intended it was necessary to sit at my desk, while smoking a cigar and waiting to hear from George, and make notes on what to talk about.

Many young Russians had hinted about the lack of freedom in intellectual matters. They had little faith in the messages put out by their newspapers and journals, and imagined publications from the West to be far more free and interesting. The only newspaper available in English was the communist *Daily Worker,* and though it was often far less rigid when it came to the party line, they didn't trust that, either.

They also distrusted critics and academics who told them what it was healthy under the system to believe. Translated novels by foreign writers always had an introduction telling them how to interpret what they were about to read. The hatches of censorship seemed more onerous than I had thought they were in the summer. Yet the young, always hopeful, only wanted their country to allow greater freedom in the arts and humanities, assuming that when this came about real civilisation would exist.

I had mentioned to various editors the case of Daniel and Sinyavsky, as well as that of the student who had received three years in prison for organising a demonstration, but had no success in drawing them out.

In my luggage were books by myself and other writers, to give away, yet I couldn't help wondering why the authorities were so tightfisted in not buying them for their students, and other members of the public. I supposed they didn't want their readers to become influenced by liberal ideas but also, if such books were imported, they were afraid of the murderous rush to get at them in the shops.

At dinner in the Writers' Union George introduced me to the poet Alexei Zaurikh, with the words: 'Meet a famous foreign writer.'

We'd drunk a good deal, and Zaurikh exclaimed: 'Hey, he

can't be a foreign writer. He looks just like one of us, who belong to the Moscow hooligans.' As he came forward to give the usual bear hug George said: 'No, he's not. He's one of the Nottingham hooligans,' at which everyone, including me, had a good laugh, and went back to the bottle.

Saturday, 9 September
I had always thought that aspiring writers would be much better off teaching themselves by trial and error, if need be, rather than listening to professors and already successful authors telling them how it should be done, and yet here I was, about to do the same.

I was shown on to a dais, wondering what those hundreds of young people expected me to say on opening my mouth. Two officials of the establishment bracketed me, and since I also wore a tie I didn't suppose the audience of mostly students thought there was much to choose between us, and that I would bring out the same old party line. I was expected to sit but preferred to stand, at which a flunky immediately levered the microphone to my level.

After the usual hesitations I launched into what I was clearly not expected to mention, to the obvious unease of the dean and his sidekick. How much the audience understood was hard to say, though I'd been told that many would know English.

After taking a few minutes to inform them of my origins and how I became a writer – establishing my 'working-class' credentials, though on this occasion I decided not to be bashful about that – I went on to say that writers should have the freedom to write what they felt inspired to say, in other words whatever they liked. It was futile and certainly unnecessary to clothe them in straitjacket theories of social realism.

Demanding literature of that or any kind was a barrier to creativity. A writer should be left to develop his own personal idiosyncratic style, and tackle any subject that came to mind, without having to consider what an audience might want. Complete liberty in these matters would eventually give birth to a literature that in the end would be of more value, and even more patriotic, if you like, but certainly more credit to his country than if any obstacles had been placed in his way.

Young writers should be permitted to experiment with form and style if they wanted, and have a chance at least of getting published. If the worst came to the worst, and no editor wanted it – as often happens of course in the West, where my work went around for ten years before anything was taken – he can always put it away for a year or two, and wait his chance, meanwhile writing something else. But whatever transpired he should keep on writing, and hope that one day he would get into print somehow. Did not the great Tolstoy say to Maxim Gorki (who would surely have agreed with what I am saying) 'Don't let anyone influence you, fear no one, and then you'll be all right'?

Before going on to mention the writer's justifiable dissatisfaction with any forms of censorship I said something about theatrical and cinematic censorship in England. I told them of the fight with the British Board of Film Censors, when Karel Reisz and Tony Richardson had been forced to show them every draft of *Saturday Night and Sunday Morning* and *The Loneliness of the Long Distance Runner*. We had been compelled to make amendments through every turn of the script, which were unjustified and unnecessary, but there had been no other way to get the films made.

Such information now seemed to be received with approval by the men at my side, who no doubt told themselves what else could you expect in the capitalist West? But then I went onto the offensive on censorship in all countries, including the one in which I was speaking. Having asked me to talk during my pre-paid hard-currency holiday they could hardly hold it against me for not talking like a specially invited all-found guest.

What I want for myself, I informed them, I not unnaturally desire for all writers everywhere. We must stand united in that if nothing else. In conclusion I praised the poems of Andrei Voznesensky, since he was in trouble with the authorities at the moment.

I wasn't disappointed by the decibels of applause at the end. George gave his usual louche wink, and discreet thumbs up, which was good enough for me as we went out. He later said that my speech had been much appreciated, and that the gist of it was all over Moscow by evening – among those to whom it mattered.

Sunday, 10 September
On my way to visit a Russian family, whose address had been given me in London, I turned a corner and saw a man, wearing a blanketlike overcoat – his fur hat nearby – spreadeagled between the pavement and the gutter. Deader than a dead man could ever have looked, he might have hit the deck from twenty floors up, and landed in such a posture that had he performed a similar collapse of all faculties in a ballet at the Bolshoi the whole audience would have been on their feet in a fever of applause and appreciation. As it was he had merely taken refuge in a little death from the too great strain of modern life – unless it was only to soothe the turbulence of his soul as in the old days.

In other words, he was blind drunk, and to go by his features he was one of the sub-proletariat. I could only say good luck to him in his blacked-out condition. In tsarist times he would have been thought of by the intelligentsia as one of the 'dark people' they were trying to save, though I supposed there to be marginally less of such nowadays, and that whoever fitted into that category had a love-hate relationship with the Soviet system – love because of indisputable benefits, and hate for having been dragged into an existence of stricter discipline. I assumed he would totter off sooner or later, and went on my way.

Walking up the steps to the flat I found the correct nameplate and rang the bell. After some wait I buzzed whoever was inside several more times. The block was cleanly kept, with no sign of broken bottles.

No one was in, the place so quiet I didn't think there could be anyone in the other flats either. They were all out for the weekend maybe, or the people I had come to see thought it unwise to open the door and receive the small gift in my haversack I had been asked to deliver.

On my way back to the centre of town, annoyed at not having accomplished my mission, I saw that the drunken man was no longer where he had been, though the curving river of urine still mapped the pavement. The militia must have bundled him into a van and taken him away for deintoxication which, I had been told, was the usual procedure.

Moscow wasn't built to a scale for walking, like Paris, London, or Madrid. On the other hand a unique and efficient Metro served all areas. The grand and sombre city impressed rather than welcomed, and it was easier to give oneself up to it more than feel much affection. I supposed it inspired loyalty and even love for those who lived there and had overcome its sense of intimidation, and their own insignificance. St Isaac's Cathedral in the distance would have seemed more pleasant to reach if the space in front of me was covered by a maze of streets.

I went with Oksana to a peasant market near the Moscow River, where people with string bags and briefcases were scooping up much that was on offer. I wanted to buy a couple of Orenburg shawls for Ruth which were made from goat's hair, said to be so fine they could be drawn through the space of a wedding ring. The woman with battered teeth showed how this could be done, then wrapped them up as if not too happy to let them go. We left her trying to get the ring back on her finger.

Oksana wondered if I wanted any souvenirs to take home, but I said I already had enough *matrioshka* dolls to cover a table. Back in Red Square she asked if I would like to go inside Lenin's tomb. 'Everyone does.'

'Look at that long queue, though. I wouldn't get in till tomorrow.'

'Oh no,' she said, 'you can walk in straightaway, as a special guest.'

I didn't care to see the embalmed Lenin. What could his body mean to me? He was dead already, wasn't he? 'Perhaps we'll see it some other time,' I said, to her disappointment, as if she might have liked another look at it.

Monday, 11 September

Russia is a difficult country if you don't speak the language, or want to send a telegram, or travel on the Underground, or dine at a place where the menu is printed or written by hand only in Cyrillic, but no problems are insurmountable, or so I supposed when, to save time, I went alone to draw 500 roubles from my savings.

The huge building housing the bank was on Gorki Street,

and the more I looked at its palatial structure the less sure was I of being able to make the transaction. Dozens of counters in the grand though somewhat intimidating hall were each for a different sort of business, and I walked behind people filling in forms trying not to appear as if casing the place for a robbery, looking at my passbook in the hope of finding a word corresponding to one above a particular counter. I felt foolishly conspicuous, though no one took any notice. The atmosphere was stuffy and hot, and I had to be back at the hotel soon and meet George, who would take me to explore the Kolomenskoye district.

Coming to what seemed a possible place, I was told to fill in a white form from a pile by the opening. Setting my briefcase down, and pulling out my fountain pen, I inscribed name, address, serial number of bankbook, the date of issue, and the amount to be extracted, then sent the completed form through the pigeonhole to the woman clerk. I stood by to await results.

Such simple business should have been as easy as in any other country, but I was wrong. She eased the book back, jabbed her finger at the form on top of my passport, and said something I didn't understand. She smiled at least, pointed further along the hall, and went back to shifting her beads from side to side of an abacus frame.

I guided my briefcase to the next *guichet* with my feet, and was given a blue form from the pile and told to fill in that as well. The last place must have been for depositing money, and now I was at the right one. Sweating with concentration I picked out the salient words, and did a tolerable job on that chit also, even managing my name in Russian script under the English version. Proud of my accomplishment I wondered whether it shouldn't have been written above, a minor infringement, but it might have been sufficient reason for the woman banishing me to another position. Too late now. I handed the form through as if giving my first novel to a publisher, because back it came, I didn't know why but, keeping the two forms in my hand I went to the next place along, by now fully engrossed in their dour game of 'pass the tourist'. A woman with a briefcase and shopping bag stood before me and, without my asking, paused from filling in her own form and handed me another to complete. I set to work, weary from having to deal with so much bullshit, and hoping that matters would now accelerate.

A hopeful sign was that actual money was being counted for the woman in front. Meanwhile I wondered about her status or profession, but didn't get many clues before she went away. Grateful that she did so without taking time to check her cash, I pushed the blue form, plus the others filled in, as well as my bankbook, passport, and driving licence for good measure across the wood.

A motherly figure, wearing steel spectacles, her grey hair in a bun – much like the other women clerks – she flattened the bankbook, after a glance at my passport, fingered through a file box to her left, and lifted out a card which must have had my details on it. She stamped other entries in the book, which I later discovered took care of interest. I admitted to myself that things were now going well. 'I've read your novel,' she said. 'How much money would you like to take out?'

I had written the amount three times, but supposed she wanted a chat during her monotonous work. I wedged the money into my wallet and wished her farewell. Worn out, though the day had hardly begun, I went off to find George.

I was asked to lunch by an American from the Associated

Press who, having his ear sufficiently to the ground, had heard something of what I had said in my lecture, so wanted to interview me. He was good at his job, and knowledgeable about goings-on in Moscow. We talked awhile, correctly assuming that I needed him as much as he needed me.

In any case I invariably got on well with Americans, being old enough to appreciate what their nation had done for the rest of us during the Second World War. It was true of course that the Soviet Union had borne the brunt of the fighting, but I had never, as with the majority of other left-wing people, uttered the infantile cry of 'Yanks Go Home'.

Over the excellent meal he asked if I agreed with Graham Greene, who recently said that royalties from his books, which could not be taken out of Russia, should be given to Daniel and Sinyavsky who were now in prison, and their works banned.

I recalled that before leaving London the BBC Russian service asked me to say a few words about the matter, but I turned them down knowing I would shortly be able to make my views known on native ground. At the same time I wondered why no one from the BBC had phoned me a few years before to talk about Christopher Logue and Bertrand Russell who had also been sent to prison for their beliefs.

I had no hesitation in telling the American that I would be only too glad to donate whatever was available of my royalties to the two writers behind bars for the wrong reasons, and hoped they would soon be released. As we ate and drank I came out with much more, but nothing I didn't want to be recorded.

Tuesday, 12 September
An article in the *Daily Worker* gave an undistorted account of what I had said to the American. This was much to its credit.

Other Western newspapers carried reports, but they didn't concern the authorities since they weren't on sale for people to read.

The *Daily Worker* was a different matter, and from then I was pestered – there's no other word for it – to write an article for *Pravda*: only a short one. 'Just say something about not believing in what you said, or that you were misquoted, or your words were maliciously taken out of context, or even that you hadn't said such things at all.'

I played innocent and naïve, as if not knowing what they were getting at, and denied nothing. I was my own man. I was on holiday.

Wednesday, 13 September
In the evening I was invited for drinks at Valentina Ivasheva's. We toasted Russia – as who would not? – Uncle Dima joining in with a smile hard to describe, though he was no fool, and knew what I had done. Valentina gave a few leery and almost pleading looks, but maybe she was afraid to tax me directly in case I showed my true proletarian colours and broke a few bottles in the vestibule on leaving. I knew what was troubling her, but had no intention of getting into a discussion.

Later, at Tanya Kudraevzeva's – who worked for *Foreign Literature Magazine* – I got on well with the young people, all of us relishing the food and drink of the party. One or two who realised I would be leaving for London in the morning still badgered me to recant.

About midnight I stood in a group by the lift door waiting to go down to street level, and though more people could fit comfortably inside, a young writer was pushed in so that we two could descend together. When the door closed he said: 'Please don't deny anything in the article about Daniel and Sinyavsky.'

I patted him on the shoulder. We may have been slightly drunk, and I was surprised he felt the need to ask. 'Don't worry,' I told him. 'Nobody will get anything out of me.'

Thursday, 14 September
Even at the airport terminal Oksana wanted me to hurry off a short piece before boarding the plane. It was obvious why we had arrived an hour or so early. I looked sorry at disappointing her, and said I couldn't.

When the plane lifted from the runway the prospect of getting home and resuming work on my novel A *Tree on Fire* began to absorb me, so the problems of Russia could be forgotten for a while. At the same time I was both happy and sad for a country that had so many good people in it, and wondered when I would be able to go there again.

Part Three

A Nest of Gentlefolk
1968

9 November

Could it have been a case of 'come home, all is forgiven'? Whatever it was, Ruth and I were invited to attend the 150th Anniversary Celebrations of the birth of Ivan Turgenev. The prospect of going to Russia again was too good to miss. I had just published *Love in the Environs of Voronezh*, as well as a book of stories called *Guzman, Go Home*. Whatever else was in progress could wait awhile.

Another English writer in the group was James Aldridge, whom we had met at the Hampstead house of Ella Winter and Donald Ogden Stewart. His 600-page novel *The Diplomat*, set in the Persian region of Azerbaijan just after the Second World War, had long been popular in the Soviet Union.

We waited in the airport terminal for our luggage, till despondently realising that one of the suitcases was not going to come on to the carousel, a new experience for us – up to that time. I had visions of it being motored to the Moscow flat of a fence who would sell the contents at one of the street markets. Or it was already being loaded on to a plane for disposal in Irkutsk. Scarves and heavy sweaters were in it, and God knew what else, so it would be hard to endure the winter temperatures without them.

Oksana, with her expressive all-knowing eyes, tried to put us at our ease. 'Don't worry. The case will come to your hotel in the morning. But now we must leave, because the others are already waiting in the bus.'

At least we'd had the sense to wear our Russian fur hats, though the first touch of outside air was a knifely shock to the skin. The rest of those on board were mainly writers from communist countries, or from Latin America.

Soon after being installed in one of the 3,000 rooms of the new Hotel Rossiya, George came to welcome us. As always full of life's enjoyments, he kissed Ruth's hand like a true cavalier. And then, in his Georgian prince manner, he telephoned room service and asked them to bring champagne and caviar, aware of course that it would be paid for by the state.

We invited him to join us at dinner but he said, with the wink of an amateur conspirator, that he had a date with someone who would never forgive him if he let her down.

Sunday, 10 November

The missing suitcase did not turn up as had been promised, so we entreated long suffering and by now worried Oksana to do her best and make sure it did before we froze to death. Meanwhile we put on all the clothes we had and walked up Gorki Street with James Aldridge, glad to have a companion who knew more Russian than we did.

Back at the hotel there was still no sign of the suitcase, and I (laughingly) told Oksana in the evening that there soon would be if large notices were displayed at the airport explaining, in no uncertain terms, that unless it was found, and quickly, we would perish from the cold, and then a few baggage handlers would be sent to Siberia – or shot.

Monday, 11 November
After breakfast Oksana telephoned from the lobby saying a car
was waiting to take us to the airport, where we could identify
our case. Did that mean it had been found? She couldn't be
sure, but on arrival we were shown into a room with other
missing luggage stacked around the walls.

Ruth spotted ours right away and, on making sure no one had
opened it, we produced the identifying docket, signed several
forms in at least triplicate, and had it sent to the car.

Tuesday, 12 November
Chairman Skobelev, head of the Turgenev celebrations, asked
if I would give a short speech from the stage of the Bolshoi,
where the proceedings were to be officially opened. Mr
Brezhnev would be there, and many other Soviet notables.

When I agreed to do it Oksana said I should write the speech
beforehand and then show it to her. They were taking no
chances. I scribbled some notes, and borrowed a typewriter
from the hotel, to make the text plain for reading.

I put in a few remarks from my talk of the previous year, and
of course also mentioned what a great novelist Turgenev had
been, and how he had lived at a time when it was comparatively
easy to travel in and out of Russia, which should be possible for
writers today. The latter part of this sentence was something
that, under the circumstances, could not be used, since Mr
Brezhnev might not approve. I had expected as much, though
was told that the rest would pass all right. As a guest I agreed to
the cut, but at least won a little that was worth saying. The
speech was put into Russian by George.

Other delegates spoke – everything simultaneously translated
– and from my position on the stage I took in the greyish

unmoving features of Brezhnev in his box, seemingly bored by whatever was said, though later he enjoyed and applauded the dramatic excerpts from Turgenev's works, as well as the singing and dancing.

Wednesday, 13 November
Nothing was too much trouble to keep foreign guests busy and content. Those who made sure the hospitality was as well arranged as possible – such as Oksana – deserved our thanks. I told myself that the price to be paid was never onerous, on being asked to talk at the Writers' Union on Turgenev's novels, where I was careful to get in what had not been possible at the Bolshoi.

Their response was to say that foreign travel was not as impossible as I imagined, because Soviet writers – such as Mikhail Sholokhov and Yevgeny Yevtushenko – were often allowed abroad to give lectures and readings. This I well knew, having met them at various times in London, but I didn't consider it enough, because they were only let out under stringent conditions. I felt sorry for Oksana, who had to do all the interpreting.

George came with us to the savings bank – no difficulty for me this time – to help me take out 800 roubles from my account, which left 969 still there and never collected.

As I was folding the notes George met one of his former professors, a dignified smartly dressed elderly man carrying the inevitable briefcase and wearing spectacles. It was interesting to see so much deference, bowing and hand kissing on George's part, though he seemed to have enduring respect and affection for the old man who was very happy to receive it.

Ruth and I passed the evening with the well-known poet

Rimma Kazakova at the Writers' Club, and spent some hours talking with her about the current situation.

Thursday, 14 November

We obtained transit visas for our return journey at the Polish consulate, and did the same business at the office of the German Democratic Republic. Our plan was to go home by overlanding to Holland, for the experience of a long train journey.

We then went to Maxim Gorki's house on Kachalova Street, where he had lived from 1931 until his death in 1936. I had read many of his works, but found the last novel *Klim Samgin* impossible to get into. The suspicion had always been that he hadn't died a natural death, but was poisoned on Stalin's orders for being too outspoken against the regime – though Gorki had nevertheless supported the slave-labour project of the White Sea Canal in the 1920s.

It was an opulent residence for a writer who endured such poverty as a child and young man, comfortable and elegantly furnished in the art deco style, with many artefacts and pictures of his time. The writing desk seemed still to be glowing with use. He also had a museum to himself on Vorovska Street, in a building put up for Prince Gagarin in 1820, where books and manuscripts and much else was on show, but there was no time to see it.

At the Tetryakov gallery, the first time for us, we concentrated on seventeenth-century icons and the landscapes of Levitan. The gallery was presented to the city in 1892 by the brothers Pavel and Sergei Tetryakov, who were patrons and connoisseurs. Ten years later they gave another fifteen hundred items, and by 1914 it housed four thousand, thus earning an asterisk in

Baedeker. It now had fifty thousand paintings and sculptures, which made it a good place for the study of Russian art.

In the afternoon I kept an appointment for an interview at the hotel, but forgot what it was for no sooner had it ended. We managed half an hour's sleep, then attended the theatre with the rest of the Turgenev group. A late party at Valentina Ivasheva's went well because she seemed to have forgiven me for my outspokenness of the previous year.

Friday, 15 November
I was shown around a 'typical' Soviet school at which children learned foreign languages. Neatly dressed and smiling pupils unselfconsciously spoke a few words in clear English.

When they wanted to know what jobs I'd done in my life I mentioned that of wireless operator, which interested them more than anything else. Followed by a lady teacher I was shown into a room full of radio equipment, and very good it was. They communicated, by shortwave voice and telegraphy, with amateur clubs throughout the Soviet Union. One wall was decorated by colourful QSL (receipt of signal) cards, some from places beyond the borders of their country.

Ruth and I lunched at the Writers' Club with Boris Polevoi, editor of the influential magazine *Yunost* (devoted to youth). He it was who, in 1960, had taken a chance on publishing *Colleagues* by Vasily Aksyonov, a novel unlike any that had so far appeared in the USSR, and for that reason it became immensely popular. One knew from this that Polevoi was very much a liberal as far as new writing was concerned.

Wounds from the war had left his features slightly distorted, especially about the eyes, but he rarely failed to put on a smile when speaking. It was obvious that he worried much, and though times might be easier it was still a fight to publish what he wanted.

On my last visit to Moscow I had been told that Pasternak's great novel *Dr Zhivago* would shortly be published in Russia.

'And so we all hoped,' Polevoi said, 'and still do hope, because I'd be delighted to publish it in my magazine. What else can I say?' Students we met later at the university were in much the same mind.

Forty-five minutes before midnight a special train left from the Kursk station for Orel 239 miles to the south. The delegation would see places written about in Turgenev's novels, and the house where he had lived. Several carriages were taken up by members of the Writers' Union and other officials connected to the anniversary. Some brought their secretaries, or girlfriends and, in a few cases, their wives.

The further from Moscow the more the company relaxed, till the train seemed to have been hired for nothing less than a wild party. Ruth and I contributed a bottle of White Horse whisky, bought from a Beriozka or hard-currency shop, which the half dozen in our compartment began guzzling even before the lights of the conurbation fell behind. They had supplies of their own, especially vodka, but also Georgian wines and good things to eat.

The engine with its large red star pulsated through the dark spaces, the jollification in our carriage making a place unconnected to any other, with the clinking of glasses, laughter, and the merry compliance of the girls. Much food and booze passed between the cabins, fuelling a party in the good old Russian mode. Handshakes and backslaps for foreigners, a constant plying of liquor, and kisses for the smart and agreeable young women – even for the not so young – went on through the night.

Those in compartments who didn't care to enjoy the beverages were mostly ladies from Latin America, wanting to discuss literature or the world political situation, though how they were able to, with such fraternal comings and goings along the corridors was hard to say. The only way to be at home in any country was to drink with those who lived there, and most needed no second telling to join in, which soon put levels of self-indulgence to the test.

Saturday, 16 November
At one o'clock in the morning, with no diminishment of uproar, the train halted at a station so that goods wagons could rattle through a junction further south. The stop promised to be long and, fresh air being needed after so much carousing, I stepped on to a long empty platform thinly coated with ice.

In only a jacket, but warmed by vodka, I thoughtlessly propelled myself into a delightful slide of fifty or so yards. It was an exhilarating motion, more a reversion to childhood, as I scooted with arms spread to achieve an even longer lap, sailing like a bird from one end of the train to the other.

Unaware of providing a spectacle, till hearing applause from the windows, I might have gone on with such madcapping all night, or until I dropped, but a shriek from the engine alerted me to get back on board. The inconvenience of being left alone in the unlit space of Mother Russia made me realise that I would either freeze to death on the icy platform, or have to fend for myself among astonished people, if I could find them, who would so little know what to make of me that I would soon enough not know what to make of myself, even if I didn't already.

Leaping for the steps as the wheels squeaked into movement, my berserker antics came to an end, as did the party soon afterwards.

Shaken from a half sleep at six o'clock in Orel, and persuaded from the litter of cups, bottles, cigarette stubs and paper bags, we were led like a gaggle of walking wounded to a bus which took us to a hotel in the city.

All everyone needed was sleep, but after breakfast we were marched back to our transport, which took us to lay flowers on the Turgenev monument, then to scenes in the district described in *A Nest of Gentlefolk* and *A Sportsman's Sketches*. How much we would remember was hard to say.

Still zombie-like, we filed through the Turgenev Museum, opened for the centenary of his birth in 1918. He was the first Russian novelist to be widely known and appreciated throughout Western Europe in the nineteenth century. Most of the furniture had been brought from his country place at Spasskoye Litovinovo, while the desk and chair of his Paris study was as if waiting for him to come in from dawdling in the garden and get to work. Glass sheltered copies of translations and first editions, and works of art adorned the walls. It was fascinating to hear that the rooms had been recreated exactly as those in his country house. The Karelian birchwood and walnut Russian Empire-style furniture was made by serf craftsmen, and I hoped they had been well treated for having such skills.

Most of us began to stagger by the time we came out of the Museum of Painting, and welcomed the half hour's rest after lunch, but then for the benefit of French visitors we had to see a street named after the Normandy–Niemen squadron which had fought for the Russians in the liberation of Orel. Afterwards we went to a meeting with students to talk about Turgenev's life and works.

At the end of the evening concert half a dozen students joined Ruth and myself saying they would like to take us on a walk around the town. We had the feeling that they didn't care to be seen too openly going off with us. It was late, achingly cold, and mostly dark beyond the city lights.

Some of the group may have intended to become writers, for they complained about the number of editors, publishers' committees, scholars, and even more sinister people who demanded to see and approve an author's manuscript before it could be given the go-ahead for printing. Luckily some magazine editors fought courageously to bring out good and often controversial work (they mentioned Boris Polevoi) which then appeared in book form, since they were already popular.

We reminded them of Solzhenitsyn, Yevtushenko, Aksyonov and others, which surely showed that things had changed from the bad old days. That was true enough, they said, but your information is not up to date, because the lid is coming down again, and times are going to be more difficult.

It was cathartic for them to talk, the discussion going on through several winding miles of glum suburban areas. Whenever the lights of the town centre showed in the distance we assumed the perambulation was coming to an end, but we were steered away so that the talk could continue. There were no complaints. In fact we were flattered at having been chosen from the delegation to broach such issues.

We were still answering questions after midnight, about the lives of writers in the West. I said that while it might seem ideal to those in countries where novelists and poets were galled by the system, in the so-called Free World there were more subtle forms of censorship. It was unofficial, but publishers and editors could turn down a book whose subject matter they decided was distasteful, on the assumption that the reading public wasn't yet ready for it, or for reasons impossible to fathom. At least that had been the situation until recently, especially with film scripts. Now it was more of a lottery to get a book into print, but there was always a chance, because not all publishers thought alike. Still, I admitted, things really were changing, and it was nowhere near as bad as in the Soviet Union.

They eventually pointed out our hotel across the square, and thanked us with firm handshakes on saying goodbye. We wondered what our long talk-about had meant to them, and whether they would remember it.

Sunday, 17 November
The bus took us fifty miles northeast on a stretch of road George and I had motored along in 1967, unrecognised now because the nondescript country to either side was monochromed with snow. Beyond Mtsensk a bust of Turgenev and a finger post indicated the way to Spasskoye Litovinovo, the estate where the writer was exiled by the Tsar in 1852 for writing a laudatory obituary of Gogol.

Under a line of birch trees flocks of snow like mice made of cotton wool parted from the occasional branch and melted into the ground. The plain wooden house, where *Rudin* was written, burned down in 1906, but was later rebuilt to look as it had in 1881, when Turgenev saw it for the last time.

It was a large house, a nest of gentlefolk, painted white, with several columns along a railed terrace, but as our feet were coldly wet (or wetly cold: we couldn't decide) we were satisfied with a glimpse of the outside, knowing that the best exhibits were in Orel.

The bus took us to the station buffet in Mtsensk for lunch, hats and overcoats coming off at the abrupt change from bitter cold to the heat of warm stoves, turning us into a merry gang, as if a lever had been pulled over us on going through the door. The large windows gave much light, and the half dozen at each table watched kerchiefed and robust women in white aprons come from the kitchen with bowls of steaming boiled potatoes, platters of gherkins, dishes of soured cream, soused herring, slices of black bread, plates of butter squares and, to send it down, quantities of ice-cold vodka. No sooner had a bottle been emptied another took its place until, going by shouts and laughter loud enough to burst the windows, we seemed back in the atmosphere of the train from Moscow. The serving women showed delight at our appetites, as they replaced dishes devoured with the gusto of the starving.

Even the demure ladies from South America were coached to take a little vodka, for medicinal purposes of course, and they also were soon quite lively and red at the cheeks. Half an hour later it was plain that all we had eaten so far was only the first part, which I had thought of as being an excellent meal in itself, and more satisfying than any to be had in an expensive London restaurant, though cold and hunger, and plenty of vodka, may have distorted my judgement.

There were many nodding heads on the coach to Orel, but in the afternoon we were treated to a film show about the Red Army defeating the Germans in the war, and the subsequent liberation of Orel. More than half the town was destroyed in the fighting. The Krupskaya Library, founded in 1843, had been plundered and burned but was rebuilt and now housed half a million books.

Orel was the first big town to be liberated, and was given an artillery salute in Moscow. I recalled listening to many others on the wireless in our living room, as the Red Army went on its way to Berlin.

It was dark by the time we filed into the train for Moscow, a trip more subdued than on the journey down.

Monday, 18 November
After breakfast in the hotel we packed our cases for departure in the evening. But our stint wasn't finished yet. There was a meeting at *Foreign Literature Magazine*, to talk about what had been seen and enjoyed in Orel. Tanya Kudraevzeva took us to lunch at her flat, where we met her beautiful daughter, who danced with the Bolshoi. And just when we thought there would be nothing to do for the rest of the day we were asked to give an interview which went on for over an hour.

George and Oksana came to put us on the train for the Polish frontier at Brest Litovsk, the first stage of 2,000 miles back to London. We thanked her for having made our ten days so pleasant, then told George, wanting Oksana to hear, that we expected him to be in London soon, somehow or other. He could rely on us feasting him well, as we talked about old times.

'There's nothing I would like better,' he said, 'and I'll do all I can to keep the appointment.'

'We'll find a way,' Oksana told us.

Placenames familiar from looking at maps during the war were passed unseen: Vyazma, Smolensk, Minsk, Baranovichi, and I thought how interesting it would be to put up for a few days at each and see the sights, mix with people in the streets.

But our throughway tickets wouldn't allow it, and in any case we were tired, wanting only to get home – even though we had taken the slow way to go about it. The train bounded along swiftly enough, every turn of the wheels taking us closer to Holland.

It was so black outside that the train might well have been stationary. There were hardly any other passengers, and we sat on our own in the restaurant car for a mediocre meal. Moscow seemed months behind, everything we had seen and done gone in the mist. London was still an enormous distance away, though we longed to be there.

At Brest Litovsk, known for its treaty in 1918, when Lenin did a deal with the Germans and let down the Allies, though I don't suppose he could have done much else under the circumstances, we were ordered out of the train and told to show our passports at a nearby office. That done, we roamed the half-lit platforms looking for a place to have coffee. There wasn't one. In Baedeker's time there had been 'a very fair' railway restaurant, but travellers were better catered for in those days.

Back where the train should have been, it wasn't. The vacant space was disturbing. Imagination works overtime when faced with the possibility of misfortune. Our visas said we were to enter Poland on a specific day, which meant within an hour or two, so where was the bloody train?

There was no one to ask, even supposing we could make our meaning clear. When we tried to get to another platform a soldier signalled us to go back. Maybe if the train had been full the desolation wouldn't have been so intimidating. I regretted again having been too idle to learn more Russian. And why had we been so foolish as to leave the carriage? The train seemed to have gone without us, and the passport office was in darkness. There was no one to ask about our plight. We had been given to understand – or had we? – that there would be at least an hour's wait. Our luggage was still on board, which didn't bear thinking about, so we tried not to or, being in a state of gloom, couldn't.

Then I remembered that the wheels of the train had to be changed to the West European gauge, but that was something I assumed would be done at the platform by a crew of dwarfish cloth-capped men tinkering musically with hammers between swigs of vodka. I didn't realise the train had to be shunted to marshalling yards and the work done there. Half an hour later we saw the carriages parked further up the platform, so were spared the inconvenience of a few forlorn days in the fortress town of Brest Litovsk.

Tuesday, 19 November
At dawn the train pulled us over a long bridge into Warsaw, though we were too far north to see anything of the city. The Polish landscape beyond was misty and nondescript in its wintry cabbage-field gloom. A couple of books still unread saved us from riffling through a rack at the end of the carriage holding copies of the *Daily Worker* and *Humanité,* and booklets of tedious argument about the ideological differences between Russia and China.

We had slept little in our bunks, so at dusk it seemed to have been dusk all the way through Poland. We stretched out early, but shortly afterwards the flashlight of Polish border guards dazzled us, and we showed our passports. Half an hour later soldiers of the German Democratic Republic barked for the same reason. Then the somewhat less brusque West German police wanted to know who was coming into their country. Another sleepless night.

I suppose we must have gone through Berlin, but I don't remember, though the lights of the world were gradually turned on for our locomotive's race to the Dutch frontier – where we encountered two more sets of border police. Since leaving Moscow we'd had nothing to eat except the evening meal on the train twenty-four hours before, and our provisions basket was empty. There'd never been much in it anyway. In Moscow we'd been too busy to think of stocking up, and in any case didn't know where to shop. Delicious meals with plenty of pleasant wine would be frequent on such a grand international express, or so we had thought. Luckily a railway-employed woman at the end of the carriage brewed lemon tea on a stove in her cubicle, whenever we wanted it.

After breakfast at the Hook we dawdled an hour or so before getting on a ship for Harwich. The sea was bleak and grey – and bloody rough – but we'd had the foresight to book a cabin, so the crossing went easily. We were home by eight in the evening.

In Moscow we were given a heavy metal medallion with the head of Turgenev stamped on it, very useful as a paperweight, and to remind us of a country we weren't to see again for thirty-six years. Much happened in that time to George Andjaparidze, which affected my relationship with the Soviet Union.

Part Four

Kuznetsov
1969

Saturday, 26 July

A tape recorder on my table, the speaker turned up full (probably driving the rest of the house mad, but I didn't care) played Handel's *Messiah* or grand choruses from *Israel in Egypt*, over and over. Inspiring sounds sent the pen across blank paper, its pile decreasing day by day.

The themes of music and novel could not have been more different, for the latter was about the 'start in life' of a predatory young man from Nottingham 'on the make' in London. What began as a long short story (an oxymoron, if ever there was one) spun itself out into 500 pages. Constant invention made it untrustworthily easy to write, but it was to sell nearly 200,000 copies in all forms and languages.

Working on the second draft, the telephone morsed the usual letter M into my ear. I didn't wonder who was calling. It could have been anyone. Though my number was in the book, people thinking it wasn't often went by circuitous routes to find it, but I had always said that those whom the gods wished to drive mad they first made ex-directory.

'Alan, this is George Andjaparidze, from the Soviet Union. Remember me?'

'I certainly do. Where are you?'

'In London.'

A lifetime's wish had come true for him when the Aeroflot

wheels kissed the tarmac at Heathrow. His note of triumph was unmistakable, but tempered I thought by the shock of good fortune, as if some malign dagger of fate, or hitch in the Soviet bureaucracy, might at any time put the kibosh on his prospect of walking in the city of his dreams. He was vulnerable to superstition, Soviet upbringing nothwithstanding, or perhaps because of it, which was a mark in his favour.

Delighted at hearing his familiar voice, I invited him to come right away for lunch, and thinking he might have a problem finding the house, I drove to the Apollo Hotel in Kensington where he was staying.

Standing on the pavement to open the passenger door and let him in – doing the chauffeur act, as he called it – he smiled on recognising the same old Peter Peugeot Estate that had taken us on a happy trip through Russia two years before.

Over lunch he told us he had been chosen, out of many who coveted the appointment, to be the minder, interpreter, and general assistant to Anatoly Kuznetsov, the author known for his novel *Babi Yar*. Oksana Krugerskaya had suggested him for the job, but the casting vote had been Valentina Ivasheva's, who always helped personable young men – and what woman wasn't able to look with favour on George?

We talked about Kuznetsov's *Babi Yar*, a ravine on the outskirts of Kiev, where the Germans and their Ukrainian helpers had, in 1941, massacred 100,000 Jewish men women and children. A survivor gave details of the atrocity to Kuznetsov (though the broad outline was no secret) and he based his novel on the event. It was also the subject of a poem by Yevgeny Yevtushenko, who with Victor Nekrasov and others frequently petitioned the Soviet authorities to put up a monument to the specifically Jewish victims. Such pleas were rejected on the grounds that only Ukrainian citizens had been murdered, and so Babi Yar remained a locality of desolate waste ground. Kuznetsov had been compelled to abbreviate or exclude parts of his book before it could be published.

He had applied to come to London (not his first time abroad) to research Lenin's stay before the First World War. He needed to see the houses he had lived in, and to describe the walks he must have taken. The centenary of Lenin's birth was approaching, and a novel by the popular Kuznetsov would be a great help with the celebrations, so he had no trouble receiving permission to leave Russia for a couple of weeks.

George and Kuznetsov were in London as guests of the Society for Cultural Relations with the USSR, and had dinner with some of its members on the evening of their arrival. The following morning they went to the Karl Marx Library, where Kuznetsov presumably did some work. Back at the hotel he said to George that he wanted to trawl the strip clubs of Soho, though both had signed a paper in Moscow saying they would do no such thing. Still, George said to us, everyone who came from the Soviet Union wanted to see what it was all about, and invariably did. He himself had found Soho squalid and unexciting, but Kuznetsov enjoyed himself so much he seemed determined to go there again.

Another part of their instructions – which I learned much later – was that George had to prevent Kuznetsov from making any contact with people who had left Russia after the Bolshevik Revolution – or at any other time. He was also advised not to let him wander about on his own, though George wondered how they could expect him, a young man in his early twenties, to stop someone of forty odd and a person of great experience, from doing so now and again.

George had hoped to bring the great writer to meet us. 'I offered him the privilege, but after such a full programme in the last couple of days he wanted to spend the afternoon by himself, though I wouldn't be surprised if he isn't off to the strip clubs. Anyway, I said he should be all right on his own, but I marked the hotel on a map so that he would have no trouble finding it again. He told me to go and have a good time with you, though to give his fraternal greetings. I did point out to him that he had a blank evening next Friday, and that we could come and see you then. He thought this a good idea.'

Ruth and I agreed, and I wrote the appointment – 1 August – in my diary.

We ate, drank, smoked, and recalled good times till late in the afternoon, when I drove him back to the hotel, where he had the smallest of rooms, with a toilet and bath along the corridor. 'But since I'm in the beautiful and enchanting city of London,' he said, 'it isn't to be sniffed at.'

A couple of days later, in the late afternoon, work on *A Start in Life* had to be put aside so that we could go to Wittersham in Kent, to find out how the decorators were getting on in a house we had recently bought. Traffic was thick on the South Circular, and we had the radio going to help away the miles. I didn't normally listen in while driving in case it disturbed concentration on the road, but for some reason we stayed tuned to hear the news at seven.

On turning right from the M2, on to the arterial lane for Tenterden, we heard the startling news that Kuznetsov, instead of making a salacious perambulation of Soho, had gone into the offices of the *Daily Telegraph* and told whoever was in the conspiracy that he had no intention of returning to the Soviet Union. He asked for help with a 'safe house' until the hue and cry of his defection had faded. Among his few possessions was a microfilmed unexpurgated copy of *Babi Yar*.

Television later that night showed George escorted to an Aeroflot plane by two stalwart mackintoshed KGB men. Then came photographs of Graham Greene and myself, with the information that on searching Kuznetsov's flat in Moscow the KGB had found a quantity of letters from us, clear evidence that we had lured George from his duty fully knowing Kuznetsov would make his bid for freedom. Perhaps it was logical for them to think so in my case, since they would have known that George had been with us while Kuznetsov went for a walk planning what he had to do, though I couldn't see why they had cooked up such untruths about letters which I never wrote.

Knowing the difficulties writers faced in the Soviet Union, I sympathised with Kuznetsov's bid to get away from it all, and had to ask myself whether I would have helped him had I been approached. I was not put to the test, but knew for sure that I wouldn't have done anything to get a friend like George into trouble. We could only feel sorry for him, on the grounds that whatever else happened he wouldn't be allowed out of Russia again.

He told me his side of the story many years later in Moscow, beginning from when I dropped him off at his hotel on 26 July. After our convivial meal he took to his bed for a much needed nap. In the evening he and Kuznetsov had supper with the novelist Basil Davidson, and his wife, who were old friends of Ivasheva's. They later took their guests out in the car to see the sights of London.

Next morning Kuznetsov told George he wanted to visit Madame Tussaud's. If a secret assignation had been set up it was the perfect place, in view of what was to happen. One can imagine hilarious dodgings among the dummies so that George wouldn't see or hear, but if someone had set up a meeting he hadn't known that the exhibits were to be moved that day, and temporarily installed elsewhere. George made an effort to find out the location, but no one could tell him. His attempt went on for some time until Kuznetsov, who had a weak heart, said he was exhausted. The search was called off, and they went to the embassy for lunch, and then to the hotel for a rest.

On the 28th they were expected to dine at Jack Lindsay's, another writer. In the morning George worked on translating a play about Lenin for the BBC, which they too hoped to use for the centenary. Kuznetsov went out for a walk. When he seemed to have been away for a long time George thought he'd called on a man named Feifer whom he claimed to know. George found out later in Moscow that he was a 'Sovietologist' and none too friendly towards the USSR.

The morning of the 29th was very wet, and Kuznetsov hadn't come back to the hotel. George feared he might have had a heart attack on the street, or gone again to Soho and been mugged. He should have telephoned the embassy and explained the situation, but hesitated because he didn't want to get Kuznetsov into trouble. If he suddenly appeared for lunch and found out that his lapse was known about he would be angry at whoever had snitched on him. Kuznetsov had all along made a point of getting on close terms with George, well before their trip to London had been confirmed, and had even entertained him in his Tula flat.

At eleven o'clock he took a call from a reporter on the *Daily Telegraph*, who asked if he knew where Kuznetsov was. Smelling a very big rat even on the telephone, George responded that as far as he knew he had gone out walking. 'And in this rain as well,' for it was streaming down the window.

No sooner had the reporter hung up than George telephoned the embassy, telling them that Kuznetsov had not slept in his bed last night. He was advised to go and see them right away, but when he got there the diplomats did not seem worried. One of the secretaries gave him tea, saying that Kuznetsov was no doubt having a fine old time somewhere and would turn up sooner or later. How could he not? He was a famous and well-respected author whose books were widely bought and read. As a wealthy man he lived the good life, with a datcha in the country, a flat in Tula and one in Moscow.

That same evening – it was still raining – George went to the novelist Walter Allen's for dinner, knowing that Kuznetsov was expected as well, but he passed his absence off as a joke, saying that his charge must have got lost somewhere on his interminable walks in the footsteps of Lenin.

After eating supper they heard on the television news that Kuznetsov had been in touch with the Home Office, and requested political asylum. The kindly and sympathetic Allens advised shocked George not to go back to the hotel but to spend the night with them, since there would be crowds of reporters waiting for him, and he ought to think about what he would sooner or later have to say to such people.

George telephoned the night porter, with whom he had become friendly – they had smoked some of his Russian cigarettes together – and was told that the press were indeed waiting for him.

He went back on the Underground in a very depressed mood. It was as if a grenade had exploded under his feet. Disbelief, sensations of failure, incompetence, and above all guilt took him over. He felt bitter at Kuznetsov's betrayal of trust, not only of him but of his country as well which, in George's view, had done so much for them both.

Apart from that, how could such a terrible event have come about, on his first trip out of the USSR? Disaster was too mild a word. He would need every moral resource to face whatever might come. Above all he steeled himself into accepting full responsibility for Kuznetsov's action. Any consequences would be his, and he would endure them with the dignity of a Georgian prince which, he once told me, had been inherited from his ancestors. But he was utterly downhearted for the rest of his stay (and long afterwards) though he fought bravely not to let it show. Nevertheless, he said, they were the worst days of his life. 'I just couldn't understand why Kuznetsov had taken such a rash and fatal step.'

He was met a little way up the street by the hotel manager who, on George telling him he didn't care to meet the press at that moment, avoided the score of reporters by leading him to another entrance, and by some back stairs to his room.

At one o'clock in the morning two police officers announced themselves at George's door. They told him that Kuznetsov was now officially listed as 'missing' so they wanted details of his appearance, which George gave, saying also that he had a weak heart, and could speak no English. Polite and even friendly, they smoked George's Moscow cigarettes. 'People disappear in London all the time,' the inspector said on leaving, 'and are never found.'

Next morning, Wednesday, Secretary Chikvaidze came and took George to the embassy. George expected stormy accusations for his neglect, but the people there showed sympathy, Chikvaidze's wife comforting him as best she could. The KGB in Moscow were already demanding they get hold of Kuznetsov 'by any means', and pack him off back to Moscow, a clearly impossible task since he was well hidden by now.

Later they went to Feifer's address, hoping for clues, only to be told by a porter that he had gone to America a month ago. Back at the embassy a score of pressmen were waiting, and after discussions with the diplomatic staff it was agreed that George would face them at the hotel in the afternoon. He knew he would be taking a risk in doing this, and that every word would be weighed in the balance against his future prospects if anything anti-Soviet appeared in the papers that he was supposed to have said, but resolved that he would keep as much *savoir-faire* as could be mustered, confident by now that he could pull it off, while never losing a sense of dread.

He treated them at first with distaste, demanding to know why they were behaving so rudely in pushing microphones into his face, but gradually they became more amiable, and so did George, who answered their questions politely and at times with some humour. He talked to them for an hour and a half, and the session hadn't been as intolerable as he expected.

In the afternoon a reporter from the *Daily Telegraph*, who had stayed behind when all the others had left, got into George's room by claiming to be a traffic clerk from Aeroflot. It was impossible to get rid of him, so they went out, and talked in a bar on the Cromwell Road. At the end of their conversation the reporter said with a smile: 'There's not much more for you to do, Mr Andjaparidze, now that you're in such trouble, than join Mr Kuznetsov and also defect. Think of what will happen to you when you get back to Russia.'

Perhaps Kuznetsov had told him that anyone would jump at the opportunity to get away from the Soviet Union, and hoped George could be persuaded into doing so. If the reporter, with his malicious advice, was successful in suborning George, then Kuznetsov might feel less guilty at having broken trust with someone certain to be held responsible.

George explained to the reporter, as coolly as possible on receiving such infamous advice – which made him more angry than he would ever be willing to show, and feeling more patriotism to the USSR than at any other time in his life: 'I love my country. I've served it, and it has served me, and I'll accept whatever it decides to do with me, because I'm not the sort of scoundrel who would run away from trouble. But let me tell you what you have done to Kuznetsov by providing him with the means to desert. You have murdered him as a writer, and I suppose you're happy at having done so. Now will you kindly leave me alone?'

When the press and television publicity appeared, those at the embassy declared that George had handled the interviews far better than anyone could have expected, an opinion that preceded him home.

Shortly after he was marched on to the plane for Moscow I wrote saying how we had enjoyed his company in London. As much as we deplored the unlucky occurrence between him and Kuznetsov, we knew that it could not have been his fault: 'so don't see how you can be regarded as guilty of anything, and hope the event won't at all spoil your chances of advancement in the Soviet academic world.'

This would of course be read by the KGB, who might then know that George was not without sympathisers in his plight. The letter was intercepted somewhere along the way, because he never received it.

On his arrival in Moscow he went through a few uncomfortable hours being debriefed. He was then told to go home and write a detailed report on all that had happened, from when he left Moscow with Kuznetsov to when he was taken back on the plane. Perhaps the example of his diplomatic prose is still in the KGB archives and will one day turn up.

After handing in his account he was reproached, and probably sworn at, for having shown too much interest in strip clubs, because in leaving nothing out of his narrative he admitted that he and Kuznetsov had been to such places. The officer went on to say: 'You should have looked after that villain more carefully, and stayed with him every minute. What else do you think we sent you for?'

Towards the end of the session, his by now genial interrogator said, to George's amazement: 'Perhaps it would have been better for you if you had taken the opportunity and stayed in England as well. You'd have done better for yourself if you had.' George didn't quite know how to take it, but was relieved that they laughed together at the idea.

An ex-KGB general, Vasily Tikhonov, assistant head of the Department of Foreign Travel, later took George out to tea. He was friendly, and remarked on how competently he had handled the press interviews in London. 'You did well, young man. I really don't see how you could have done any better.'

George thanked him for the compliment, and said: 'The only thing is that I'm really having trouble with people at the university, and the Writers' Union. Some of them are treating me like shit, and making all kinds of remarks about what happened to me in London. I can't really think why, because I'm sure none of them would have done any better.'

'It's very wrong of them to be like that,' Tikhonov said. 'But you know what that sort are like. They're all afraid of losing their jobs and pensions.' He told George however, that because of

Kuznetsov's defection, he might not be allowed to go abroad again for at least ten years.

Tikhonov made a few telephone calls which stopped the spiteful behaviour at the university and other places, but slanderous rumours of George's relationship with Kuznetsov followed him around for some time. Everyone knew of the celebrated event, and in the enclosed academic world of Moscow there were speculations as to whether or not George had helped Kuznetsov in planning his escape, or done his best not to hinder him. George stood by his view that it had been impossible to divert a man from exercising his free will. Even had he followed him to the doors of the *Daily Telegraph*, and pinned him to the pavement to prevent him going in, he would have been arrested for assault, and the situation would have turned into a farce. Whoever in London had been aware of Kuznetsov's intention beforehand must have been well satisfied at having helped to bring off such a coup.

My concern was that George might believe the KGB's theory that I had played some part in the scheme by inviting him to lunch. It was chance and nothing more, and to protest my innocence in the letter to George shortly after his departure (knowing it would be read by the KGB) wouldn't have done him any good.

His prophecy concerning the errant author's future came true. I was told he lived somewhere in north London, and did work now and again for Radio Liberty. He often changed his address in case the KGB decided to have him murdered. The fact that no such attempt was made must have lowered his sense of self-importance. And considering the eruption of publicity if he had been assassinated, I can't think it was ever seriously contemplated.

Nevertheless, Kuznetsov was always careful about revealing his whereabouts, even to people who would never pose any risk, though they also could unknowingly lead those to his lair who had reason to harm him.

Someone asked a few years later if I would like to meet him, and I replied that it might be interesting to do so. I was given the telephone number, and a woman answered when I dialled. He would see me if I called again at a certain date and time. I would be informed of the address on the actual day. I put the appointment in my diary: 'Vronskaya-Kuznetsov, 17.30 hours,' but the meeting was cancelled at the last moment, and I didn't care to pursue the matter after that.

As George had surmised, he never wrote anything again. I wondered whether, as an unhappy man, he produced an account of his break for so-called freedom, though if he did, and it was published, I never heard of it. Word went around that he was disconsolate most of the time, and was drinking far too much. He died of a heart attack in 1979, ten years after he bolted.

Part Five

Consequences

From then on I was *persona non grata* not only with the KGB (of course) but with many others in the Soviet Union. A Russian writer visiting London a year or so after the Kuznetsov affair, said that at the time a Soviet publishing house was bringing out a translation of *Saturday Night and Sunday Morning*, something I'd been told before might one day happen, though I never much cared whether it did or not.

Karel Reisz, in the early 1960s, took a copy of the film version to a festival in Moscow. Madame Furtseva, the cultural minister of the time who was present at the showing, said to him afterwards that it would not be at all suitable for cinema audiences in the Soviet Union. Karel and I laughed, when he got back to London and told me about it. Who in Russia could take to a book about Arthur Seaton, who mouthed the slogan: 'All I want is a good time. The rest is propaganda!'

When I met Yevtushenko for the first time in London he showed interest in seeing the film, so I arranged a performance at a small trade cinema in Soho. He presumably didn't much like it, saying only that he had seen too many factory films already in his life.

So I'd had no illusions about the book coming out in Russia, but my informant told me that it had already been printed and bound for distribution, possibly with many cuts, I imagined, and the usual introduction as to how it should be understood.

The edition was destroyed on orders from the KGB, which organisation had much power in literary matters. I supposed the action to be a small price for Kuznetsov's freedom, and good also if some rancour at having lost their man was taken out on me instead of George. It may have had influence on his relatively civilised handling when he got home. In any case the book was, after that time, brought out in the German Democratic Republic, Hungary, Slovenia and China.

Details of what happened to George in London, and his reception afterwards in Moscow, were related by him on our meeting in 2005. He had published a book of essays, some of them autobiographical. One dealt with our trip through Russia and the Ukraine, and another described his experiences with – and without – Kuznetsov. He gave me a copy, in Russian which I couldn't read, but the inscription said: 'To Alan Sillitoe, who once upon a time called the author of this book a brother-in-arms – with old love and all the best wishes, George Andjaparidze.'

People at dinner parties in London said that Kuznetsov had done well to escape Soviet repression. He would be able to work in peace, write what he liked. That might or might not be so, I said, then reminded them of what Kuznetsov's freedom had cost George.

Yet I felt it too interesting a story not to offer more comments on the fiasco when among friends. Sometimes, without prompting and when talk flagged, I would tell about the long car journey with George, and mention how concerned his mother had been when finding him in bed with an upset stomach, after we'd eaten in a common canteen on the road from Leningrad, and she told him he ought to have had more sense than to eat in those filthy proletarian places – always good for a laugh and to lighten the atmosphere at dinner parties I rarely liked going to. I soon realised however that it wasn't right to use George in this way. The story belonged to him alone. He had earned it the hard way, and certainly wouldn't be dining out on it in Moscow – or wherever he was. He would want to forget the experience with Kuznetsov, if ever he could, and hope others would do the same, until the matter became history and he might again be able to enjoy some foreign travel.

In the years before our next meeting – a long way off – I became interested in the plight of Jews in Russia, and also said and wrote positive words about Israel and its inalienable right to exist, which divorced me from most of the left-wing people I had been friendly with before. The radical *Black Dwarf* newspaper published an article in December 1969 lauding – indeed gloating about – a Palestinian bomb attack on the offices of the El Al airline in Athens, in which an Israeli child was killed. I was enraged enough to send a letter to the editor:

Dear Sir, I originally welcomed a journal such as yours promised to be, seeing it at the time as having a useful purpose, but what worries me is your attitude to Israel, and the depradations of the so-called Palestine Liberation Movement.

I am in favour of Israel and its right to exist, and do not approve of Jewish or Israeli people being blown up while travelling in buses or sleeping in their flats.

El Fatah are tools of Arab imperialism, and its members would seem more genuinely revolutionary if they attacked those despotic medieval regimes which are only too happy to set them against Israel. I see the conflict with Israel as a frontier war between one small country and many others.

If the Arabs have a right to take Israel then the Germans and others have equal claims to go after their 'Lost Territories'.

The Israel–Palestine question is one that no British workers are interested in, but should the left-wing so-called intellectuals of the *Black Dwarf* succeed in getting them to take up the matter it might in the end make them not only anti-Zionist but also anti-Semitic. Perhaps your socialist readers are dismayed by the refusal of the Israeli and Jewish people to accept their historic role as scapegoats. You are aiding a movement that wants to make a mass Jewish grave in the sea, thus creating a solution which would be more final than any other.

My shortening of the letter still comes out as something of a screed, too vitriolic perhaps, but I wrote it in the style of the magazine in the hope that it would be better understood. When it was published in the next issue the editor stated that he disagreed with all I had said, adding that anyone who could write such trash was nothing but a racist – a common slur, then as now. I was glad when the scurrilous rag expired not long afterwards.

In 1971 I was ordered to court in Ashford for having refused to fill in the census form. My grounds were that too much was asked about people's ethnic origins and what part of the world they had came from. I didn't relish the idea of information being available to a future right-wing government which might decide to send immigrants back to their country of birth.

I paid the fine, but still didn't fill in the form, even though I could one day be provided with a free trip to Ireland, from where some of my forebears came.

I wondered how many on the *Black Dwarf* had refused to comply with the form for that reason. In June 1974 I wrote an article for *The Times* which wouldn't have been much liked by the subscribers to that paper either.

The point was that a frail middle-aged woman in Russia had, since 1962, struggled for permission to emigrate to Israel and join members of her family. A group of ladies in London had taken up her case and asked for my sympathy. Who could have refused it?

The woman's name was Ida Nudel, and in the article I compared her situation to that of a Geordie coal miner who had saved money by working double shifts and, in 1910, paid eight golden sovereigns for a passage to Canada. He had no need to ask permission, needed neither applications nor even a passport, but only wanted a better life. He went, and didn't cease to appreciate and even love his own country. When the war began in 1914 he enlisted in the Canadian Army and fought for almost four years in the worst battles on the Western Front. His country gave him liberty, and he responded with responsibility, an impossible treaty in a communist dictatorship.

After the first request to vote with her feet Ida Nudel lost her job in economic engineering, and had to do manual work for which she was in no way suited. She signed letters and petitions with others asking for the right to emigrate, took part in strikes and demonstrations, and helped those who also dared to ask for exit visas.

Repeatedly arrested, she was sent to Siberia for four years, living in conditions unsuitable for all but the most robust. Back in Moscow, she was exiled to a town near the Rumanian border, hundreds of miles from her home. Even there, though ill, she was continually harassed by the police.

My article could have brought little comfort to the Soviet authorities, but whether it was any help to Ida Nudel I couldn't say, for some time elapsed before she was allowed out – but leave she did.

Anticipating that happy event I wrote *The Interview*, a one-act play in which someone like her is brought before a Soviet officer of the emigration services to talk about her most recent application for a visa. The piece was put on at St Martin in the Fields, Janet Suzman taking the part of Ida. Not many people attended, though I was asked to talk about the matter on the BBC.

At about the same time I was shown a flysheet advertising a discussion to be conducted by graduates and teachers of the University of London Union. David Mercer, the playwright (who was also sympathetic to Israel), and myself, were accused of being 'traitors to the English working class'. The paper explained, in Marxist baby talk, why they thought so. Their reasons were amusing, though I was alarmed that supposedly educated people could believe in such rubbish without blushing. God help the students who had types like that for their teachers.

The Interview was later put on at the Almost Free Theatre in Soho, and I took more interest this time by going to rehearsals. The actor who was to play the interrogating colonel quibbled about certain of my phrases on the grounds that they were difficult to say, but my feeling was that he thought them too anti-Soviet – though I may have been wrong. The facts were so incontrovertible that it made little difference, and the full text was to be published anyway.

Those were the days when international pressure against Israel was increasing, though one wondered when it hadn't been. Anti-Zionism was (and still is) the fashionable thing, whether or not it is a country always in peril from surrounding neighbours. I went with Stephen Spender to Paris to protest about Israel having been voted off the UNESCO cultural organisation. Spender and I spoke our views, then had an excellent meal together in the Eiffel Tower restaurant.

A year later I went to a conference in Brussels dealing with the plight of Jewish 'prisoners of conscience' in the Soviet Union, and spoke at that too. Golda Meir was there, and I forget what we said to each other, but not much because she was so busy, our introduction little more than a handshake. A further conference in Paris took place a little before Israel was voted back into the UNESCO organisation.

Some of all this must have filtered through to Valentina Ivasheva in Moscow, because in talking to a British academic (who reported back) she remarked that I was nothing more than 'a Zionist agent'. Such flattery was repeated in a Hungarian magazine, and perhaps others, though that was the only one I knew about, pointed out to me by a Hungarian who worked for the BBC.

I recalled another comment of Ivasheva's about Pamela Hansford Johnson in Russia with CP Snow. She had written in one of her novels that when they were in Moscow there were 'bugs' in their room. Valentina was outraged on reading this, saying that there were no such insects in Soviet hotels. What Pamela had meant, of course, was that the room was bugged, that it had concealed microphones to hear the conversation of the guests.

Another anecdote was about John Wain and John Braine. The first John was invited into the latter John's room for a drink, but Wain told Braine to keep his voice down and be careful what he said because the place was bugged. Big, bluff, outspoken Yorkshireman John Braine was having nothing of this, and on asking where they were went over to the nearest picture, behind which the mike was no doubt concealed, and bellowed: 'If you're listening to us you know what you can do, don't you? You don't? Well let me tell you. You can FUCK OFF!' He then strolled back to John Wain and said: 'We'll be all right now. We can just say what we like.'

It was easy to see why Valentina was disappointed, even offended, by my activities but, perhaps strangely enough in those years, countries of the Soviet Bloc occasionally invited me to their parties and receptions. Ruth and I were even awarded – shall I say? – a week in the German Democratic Republic, memorable because I met Günther Klotz. His translation of *The Loneliness of the Long Distance Runner* was reputedly so good that it became the only German version used.

We talked a long time in his flat, and he told us that, having himself come from a 'bourgeois' family he'd had much prejudice to fight. People were nurtured and given all the best jobs if they came from the 'proletariat', no matter what their intelligence or eligibility. That was disgraceful and stupid, I said. 'Any country which abandons merit and relies blindly on "class" will in the long term be doomed.'

After the unification of Germany I received a large royalty cheque for the many copies of my books sold while the German Democratic Republic existed. None had been cut or censored either, so I can say thank you very much, for it's more than I can say for Russia and other East European countries.

The Hungarians and Czechs printed one or two of my stories in magazines, and I was asked by the Bulgarian cultural attaché to translate work by their national poet Hirsto Botev (1848–76), which I did. More surprising was when my novel *A Start in Life* was serialised in *Foreign Literature Magazine* in Moscow, and I received a certain amount of money for that. Perhaps I wasn't so much out of favour after all.

Still, I wondered what had been done to it. My novel *Key to the Door*, published in the early 1960s, came out in an edition of two million copies, which would have earned me a tidy sum had the Soviet publishers abided by the Berne Convention. Cuts, however, had reduced the original 500 pages by a third, and I found out why when Adelheid Fandry, a young woman from Hamburg University, came to see me. She had made the translation from English into Russian the subject of her thesis, so gave an interesting breakdown on what had been inadmissible in the Soviet Union – nothing very surprising.

I continued to meet Russian writers in London. With Ruth Fainlight, Ted Hughes and others, I went to Yevtushenko's performance at the Commonwealth Institute in 1979, and he all but mesmerised the full hall by his dramatic recitation. In some ways it was outlandishly hectoring, even had a sort of bullying tone, well developed I supposed after so many appearances in front of Russian audiences, who traditionally liked that sort of thing. On my first trip to the USSR I had bought a record of readings by Mayakovsky and Yesenin reading in the same mode.

Unlike British poets Yevtushenko knew his work so well he had no need to look at a text, everything going into the impressive delivery.

We went to a restaurant for supper, and on our way in he detached himself from, the others and, embracing me in the Russian fashion said, close to my ear: 'Keep it up, about the Jews.'

I couldn't understand the necessity for secrecy, though did

not expect him to bawl it out either. But his tone was as if wanting me to know that we were in the same underground club together, and that it was inadvisable to let anyone hear his exhortation, which might get one of us – though him most likely – into difficulties.

In the restaurant he endeared himself to everyone, even those not of the party, with his uninhibited behaviour, generously ordering champagne and handing it around.

On 28 May 1981 George telephoned me from his hotel in London, and we made arrangements to meet, though not for lunch. I was surprised he hadn't been told to give me a wide berth, though even if he had it wouldn't have worried him. In any case I had already been to several gatherings at the flat of the Russian cultural attaché and his wife, and had been invited to celebrate the anniversary of the Revolution at the Soviet Embassy. During that party someone said you must meet the Lord Mayor of Nottingham, and I thought why not? There he was, with all the glittering tin of regalia on his chest as I put out a hand to shake. Maybe I'd had a few by then, though to my regret only wine was served, but he drew back on hearing my name, and wouldn't greet me. I suppose he thought my books had given his city a bad name.

We saw George only twice, for he was a busy man. He came to dinner with us and the film maker Mira Hammermesh, and then we took him to a reading at Bernard Stone's bookshop. He was eleven years older, and a little more corpulent, as became the director of a large Soviet publishing house that had sent him on business to a London that didn't have the same atmosphere of doom as before.

I was glad to see a renewed and confident man of substance who had made something of himself after the disaster of 1969.

He was happy to be in England again, having a genuine love for the country which never left him.

The only mention of Kuznetsov was when he chided me for remarks I'd made at a certain dinner, when I should have kept my mouth shut, which were taken up by a journalist and published in a local paper.

The friendship resumed its old intensity on talking about our marathon motor trip, one of the good times of his life, as it had been of mine. We were much older, and though there couldn't have been the same sense of intimacy as before, it was to rekindle when we met again in Moscow for the last time, after the fall of the Soviet Union.

Part Six

The Last of George
2005

Saturday, 7 May

Getting up at half past seven was far too early, but that had always been the case when setting out on a journey. I was looking forward to seeing Moscow again, and in the intervals of our work for the British Council hoped to meet up with George Andjaparidze. My novel *Moggerhanger* was going the rounds to find a publisher, so a break from the hard slog was welcome.

The hire car came on time at ten, and standing at the door I noticed a strong west wind, which meant our plane would have a well-assisted take off into it, and a good push at the tail on turning east.

The couple of hours' wait in the departure lounge could have been better spent in bed, for the plane wasn't scheduled until 13.20. Ruth read the paper, while I went to the smoking area, noting a fine day beyond the sealed windows, and hoping we'd have similar weather in Moscow.

We boarded the plane at the set time, but were still on the perimeter track forty minutes later (with apologies for the delay) till the captain saw a green light from the control tower, or however it was done these days, and rocketed his full bus above the clouds. The familiar conurbation was soon out of sight and, after a tolerable British Airways lunch, I dozed, for there was nothing to see but sky.

Three and a half hours later the plane descended to

Domodedovo airport, and after the routine of police and customs – quicker than in Soviet times – we were met by Margarita from the British Council, who had a car waiting.

The thiry-kilometre drive through rain to the city seemed endless and depressing. Among blocks of flats well off the road was much new development, something of a change from years ago.

The newish Novotel compared well with places stayed at before. Though not so close to the city centre it was comfortable, and modern in the Western style, with bathrobes, bed slippers and other such items in the room. I supposed it cost quite an amount, which was fair because we were receiving no fees for our appearances. It was, on the other hand, a privilege to be in Moscow, and would turn out doubly so if we could meet George again.

Sunday, 8 May

I didn't sleep more than a couple of hours due to glasses of black tea foolishly drunk very late, though the difference in longitude may have had something to do with it. I was up by eight local time, and we met our guardian angel Margarita who came with a car.

Having a free day (the same old sabbath) we went to the new Tetryakov Gallery and spent some hours at a special exhibition called *The Jack of Diamonds*, a recreation of one held just before the First World War, with paintings and exhibits of the period, avant garde then, and still of much interest now.

We had planned an excursion to the Sparrow Hills (asterisked in Baedeker) which would have given a historic view of the city, but we'd already had enough driving in Moscow traffic, so voted with our wheels and asked Margarita to take us back to the hotel. This was just as well, since it was niagaring with rain and we wouldn't have seen anything of the famous panorama. Back in our room I had a ninety-minute sleep.

We went to have supper with Marina Boroditskaya at her flat in one of those vast plain blocks of which there must be hundreds in this megalopolis. We took to this lively, dark-haired and good-looking woman immediately. Although it was our first meeting, Marina and Ruth had been in contact by e-mail for the past few years in connection with the anthology of contemporary Russian women poets, edited by Valentina Polukhina, and published by Daniel Weissbort in *Modern Poetry in Translation*, the periodical he and Ted Hughes started in the 1960s. Although Ruth does not read or speak Russian, the editors persuaded her to work from literals they would supply.

One of her three allocated poets was Marina. A distinguished translator of English poetry, including Chaucer, Donne and Kipling, she was able to send Ruth versions of her own poems which needed little alteration. The two of them became good friends by correspondence. Later, Ruth translated other poems by Marina, some of which were published in English magazines, and Marina's translations of Ruth's two long poem sequences *Sugar-Paper Blue* and *Sheba and Solomon* appeared in the important literary journal *Foreign Literature Magazine* and in *Novaya Yunost*. During our visit the two of them read the poems in both languages.

Having been told I liked vodka with my food Marina generously provided it. We talked about Russian culture, civilisation and history, and social conditions of the present. Many advantages, such as education and health care, affordable housing and transport available to ordinary people in Soviet times had been lost, she said, yet there had been some gains.

Maybe the shark-like winners of the battles in the new era of capitalism would eventually settle down, and bring even a fraction of their blatant prosperity to those who needed it far more.

Marina was divorced from her husband, the poet and translator Grigory Kruzhov, and shared the flat with Sergei, their twenty-year-old son, whose older brother drove us back to the hotel at midnight.

Monday, 9 May

I woke at eight-thirty after a good sleep, showered and made tea. While waiting for Marina in the lobby after breakfast I watched the march past in Red Square on television, comemmorating the Soviet victory in Berlin at the end of the Second World War.

Soldiers in Red Army uniforms of the time marched by the plinth with Thomson machine guns sloped across the chest, some carrying banners and insignia of various military units. There were T-34 tank men wearing black uniforms and padded headsets. Utility-style lorries laden with standing veterans waved red carnations at President Bush, Chirac, and other heads of state – Blair not among them.

After a wet morning the weather turned fine because, it was said, aeroplanes of the air force had been sent up to seed the clouds around Moscow, and now it was beginning to work.

We walked along the traffic-free Arbat Street where fit old gentlemen with medals and decorations promenaded in sober festival best after their appearance in the Red Square parade, one-time soldiers of the campaigns that had put an end to German Nazism. The Soviet people had suffered more than those of any other Allied nation.

Now and again someone would ask permission to photograph

one of the resplendent men, requests agreed to with modesty and dignity, yet without a smile, as if fully aware of the importance of what they had once done, and knowing that such reminders might never come again. Some of the veterans had boys and girls with them – though rarely hand in hand – who looked on grandfather with admiration and wonder, perhaps not having realised before what heroes they had been in the war. The children carried the flowers which passers-by gave to show their appreciation.

An elderly woman who had also seen active service (there were many of them as well) had a large bosom plastered with decorations. When asked to pose for a photograph she did so with a musical laugh, while making sure that her hair was in place, as a platoon of smart young soldiers in modern uniform marched past behind a band, people following and bystanders applauding.

We lunched at a nearby cafeteria, one of a chain called Moo-Moo, convenient and good to eat at. They were also, Marina said, very democratic, in that people of all sorts went to them. Back on the Arbat we bought souvenirs for our grandchildren, including a hammer-and-sickle hat for one of the boys.

That evening we went to an anniversary concert at the Tchaikovsky Auditorium. Shostakovich's 'Leningrad' Symphony, No. 7 was the star item in a programme of celebration, such a sublime and moving performance that I knew I would never hear it played so heart-rendingly again. After the first movement everyone in the crowded theatre stood for a minute's silence, in remembrance of the so many million dead – and so much misery. Others as well as myself had tears on their cheeks before the music resumed. At the finale the applause went on and on, as if the following silence would be too much to bear.

After such a moving experience it was hard to take any more, so we left the concert hall and stood in the square outside for what could be seen of fireworks from the Kremlin. Hundreds of people cheered at each technicolor shellburst of blues, greens, and spectacular floral reds.

Tuesday, 10 May
'Again in the Metro with Marina' seemed like the refrain of a song, though from what era I couldn't say. This time she took us on a tour of the most interesting stations, many built during the worst years of the 1930s. Construction went on even in the Second World War, when the Germans were within thirty miles of Moscow. Stops were further apart than in London, but each underground hall was decorated by examples of Soviet art and sculpture. One like a vast ballroom was lit from chandeliers, no spot of dust visible in their soothing light.

At the Tetryakov station we were met by the poet Glyeb Shulypriakov, a friend of Marina's, whom Ruth had talked to in London a year ago at the launch of the anthology of Russian women poets. He led us on a walk through the old Merchants' Quarter, now a residential and business area but with many of the original buildings and churches preserved. He had a flat in one of the houses, where we had tea and discussed poetry – what else?

Later, on our way back to the hotel, a man on the packed Metro offered me his seat. He was so generously persistent that I sat down, although I felt no need to. When people flowed out at the next station he took the place by me, saying he had been to Liverpool as a sailor. There was much he wanted to add but couldn't, and I knew how he felt. His face was a portrait of frustrated intention to speak. Neither was my Russian good enough, except to say how beautiful Moscow was. He searched one pocket after another to find something he could give me as a memento of our meeting. Perhaps he imagined I was one of the veterans from England (I hoped not) but he found a small wrapped sweet and, his face shining with happiness, presented it to me. We shook hands several times and I got a bear hug – as if we'd had a vodka or two – before he went out.

We took a whole week more or less out of Marina's busy life, but she was indefatigable on our behalf. At five that afternoon she came to the hotel so that she and Ruth could go over the poems they would present at the Bookberry, a large bookshop well known for poetry readings. I sat in the lobby for a smoke, waiting for the British Council car to take us to the event. Until it began I walked the well stocked and laid out shelves, with many foreign titles in Russian, and some in the original languages. But pop music wailing throughout made contemplation and browsing difficult.

Ruth and Marina had such a large audience that a search had to be made for extra chairs. *Sugar-Paper Blue*, with its theme of Akhmatova in Leningrad, went down well.

We were then driven to the place for my performance. I couldn't fix exactly where it was in relation to anywhere else in the city, in spite of having a modern and accurate street plan. I had never, as a passenger, been able to look at a map without feeling car-sick.

When a man on guard at the door asked if I would like some vodka I said yes, certainly. Taking an unlabelled bottle from under his table he bubbled two good measures into paper cups.

I opened the talk by saying that the writer is essentially a communicator, between himself and whatever readers he might be lucky enough to have. Then I gave an example of communications in one of my jobs before I had thought of becoming a writer, as a wireless telegraphist, sending and receiving messages between myself and aircraft flying from Darwin to London. To break the ice – it nearly always does – I brought out my Morse key and oscillator, and tapped a short telegram of goodwill to the audience, saying beforehand that if an amateur radio operator or ex-Marconi man among them could transcribe what was sent, I would give him (or her) a signed copy of my latest novel. No one won the prize. The only time anyone had was in Rostock some years ago, when an ex-ship's officer deciphered the words correctly

I read a condensed part of my novel *The German Numbers Woman*, with a resumé from Marina; then, after a few poems, talked more about life as a writer. The session ended with questions at ten o'clock. We went on to a Ukrainian restaurant with Anna Genina, the charming director of the Moscow British Council office.

Wednesday, 11 May

We were expected at the studio of Radio Kultura for interviews at ten, and got there well on time, but the dragon of a woman guarding the door of the building said we didn't have proper identification. She was only persuaded to let us in after a stern call from upstairs.

The round table discussion of our life and work was skilfully guided by the young presenter, and went on for almost two hours, before our 'business lunch' at a place called Pal Joey's.

With barely time to change at the hotel we were motored to a conference at *Foreign Literature Magazine*. Their offices weren't as opulent as in Soviet times, when every issue sold millions of copies. Even so it had a circulation of several hundred thousand.

The editor in chief, Alexei Slovesny, and a dozen members of the editorial staff, asked us about the state of fiction and poetry in England, and whether we could recommend anything that might be suitable for their readers. Ruth mentioned the names of several poets which were new to them. They seemed well enough informed about contemporary English fiction, knowing the titles and authors of many recent novels. They hadn't however heard of John King's books such as *England Away* and *The Football Factory*, so I explained briefly what they were about.

The discussion, with tea and biscuits, lasted until half past four, when we were ferried to the British Council offices. We had tea again, and walked from there to the Library of Foreign Literature, where a good-sized audience awaited us for another reading.

Then I spotted George, sitting slightly apart by the wall. I had asked about him several times already, and Marina dialled his old telephone number, but no one had answered to the name of Andjaparidze. This didn't surprise me, for his mother and aunt with whom he had lived must have been long dead. My only hope was that news of our visit would get around, and he would turn up at one of the venues.

Now he had. He could hardly stand, tried, but I asked him not to persist. He held up his two sticks saying he could only walk properly with them. He was in pain, and looked older than his sixty-three years. His daughter, who accompanied him, told us he mustn't stay out late, because he was quite ill. George said she was religious in the Orthodox way, and always made sure he was all right when he went out – being a dutiful (and beautiful) daughter. Because of the crush, and the uncertainty of what would happen afterwards, we arranged to meet the following night. He said we would have much to discuss.

Ruth and I read, with Marina translating, more or less a replay of the previous evening. From there we went to a party at the flat of James and Kim, of the British Council, where we were so entertained I gave them a signed copy of the book that hadn't been claimed at the Morse competition the night before.

Thursday, 12 May
While waiting for Marina to come at eleven I sat in the lobby and wrote to the English-language *Moscow Times* saying how much I had enjoyed being in the city for the recent celebrations. My only surprise – and disappointment – was that Tony Blair had missed the most important date in European history of the last sixty years. Bush, Chirac, and fifty-seven other heads of state had been present. Putin said in a speech that Russia, the United States and France were the Allies of the century, a significant slur on the British prime minister for his absence. Blair had sent Prescott instead, but he had been pushed a little behind the others on the podium in Red Square, as a hint of general displeasure. We left for home before knowing whether or not the *Moscow Times* had published my letter.

It rained most of the time we were in Moscow, so it was good that the Metro was only a hundred yards beyond the hotel entrance. From Polyarkov station we splashed through puddles with Marina for half a mile or so to the factory outlet of a shop which sold the equivalent of Ordnance Survey maps of most parts of the former Soviet Union.

I had always thought that one of the first signs of democracy was when ordinary people, and foreigners as well, could buy detailed topographical maps of their country. Now, for the first time since tsarist days, it was possible in Russia. Such maps had been top secret documents in Soviet colleges and I was told by a former geology student that when issued for instruction and research he had been threatened with Siberia if he lost them.

A middle-aged woman eyed me from behind a long desk as I looked at displays on the walls and went through racks of interesting items. High-quality maps showed spot heights and contours, towns and villages in their real shapes and locations, and gave details even of cabins in forests reached only by footpath. Large-scale maps of Kamchatka and the Volga delta were available, as well as road atlases of various provinces in European Russia and Siberia. All names were in Cyrillic, but such lettering had been familiar since first learning that alphabet in my teens.

The saleswoman was livelier while totting up a thousand roubles on her calculator. I would have bought a sample of everything in the shop but space in our cases was not unlimited. I fitted the bundles into two plastic bags so that they wouldn't saturate on our walk back to the Metro.

There was a long queue at the Moo-Moo cafeteria, but some kindly person invited us into line more than halfway to the serving counters, and nobody seemed to mind.

At five – it was still raining – we were chauffered with Marina to a gallery near the British Council where there was an excellent exhibition of photographs, *Britain in World War Two*, pictures of smouldering bomb damage after air raids, women working in armaments factories or cheerily walking towards them on the street, line-of-battleships, and a Land Army girl between two enormous dray horses. A mythologised era, perhaps, but evidence all the same that Britain too had done everything of which it was capable in the common struggle.

Being asked to open the exhibition with a short speech was an honour not to be refused. After we had finished our stint at a press conference I talked for about twenty minute on life in England at that time, taking the opportunity to apologise for Blair's absence at the recent celebrations, and saying with tongue in cheek that he should be opening the show not me, though I was very glad to be taking his place – which went down well with the mainly Russian audience.

I mentioned my work as a capstain lathe operator making parts of Merlin engines for Lancaster bombers in a factory run by women and youths like me, with a couple of tool setters held back from the army to supervise. The war was still on, but ended soon afterwards, though I had already enlisted into the Fleet Air Arm. Little could I have realised, on 8 May 1945, that I would be in Moscow sixty years later for the anniversary of the great event.

I remembered that we were given the day off in the factory to celebrate. In the crowded White Horse pub that evening, with my parents and a girlfriend, we saw a hefty woman munitions worker in heavy dark spectacles doing a can-can on one of the tables, flashing her Union Jack bloomers with every high step.

In conclusion I duplicated a press report taken in Morse from our short wave receiver of the time telling the world that Hitler was dead. In those days I could read it fast enough because we had been tutored in the Air Training Corps by an ex-police wireless operator.

The performance went down well enough for me to be asked if I would repeat the message on my key in front of the television camera, and give a short interview. Chatting later with the

British Ambassador, I wondered whether he'd disliked the reference to Blair in my speech.

From then on I sat with George who, in spite of the discomfort, looked dashing and confident in his suit and bow tie. He was invited with our British Council friends to a nearby restaurant, where I split from the main group at the long table so that we could go on with our talk.

He said that the change to capitalism from Soviet power meant untold billions of roubles being sucked out of the economy, to the detriment of the country and its poor. There were many things he liked about the new life, but more than enough that he didn't. The rape of the nation by the so-called new oligarchs was something he could never forgive.

'You must remember that besides having such rapacious people around, Russia had been exhausted for nearly a century by every conceivable disaster. Even though Stalin died over fifty years ago, and the worst seemed to be over, it was impossible for us to recover because of the Cold War. When the alteration came Russia was ripe for a free for all.'

Nearly forty years had gone by since Kuznetsov had done a runner, so I knew there were many questions I could now ask, especially about what happened in London after the discovery that he was missing. George was happy enough to give details already mentioned, and allow me to take notes on his further observations as well.

We talked a long time, and at the end he told me that he lived in a more modest way than formerly, but was content with his life. He did look with some trepidation on the fact that in a week or so he would be going into hospital for a major operation. On asking what, specifically, was wrong with him he replied: 'Just about everything,' implying that it was so serious he occasionally thought he might not come out of the anaesthetic. 'I'm sure that won't be true,' I said, 'but if you don't the world will never be the same again.'

He assured me – a touch of the old sybarite – that he didn't really care, for he was still enjoying himself. In fact his love life was so well arranged that a girlfriend called on him at least once a week. As a matter of fact, he boasted with a wink, she had been at his flat that afternoon, and they had spent a few libidinous hours together during which he'd managed to make love twice.

When he was taken off in the car at midnight by his daughter I had a strong feeling that I would never see him again.

Friday, 13 May

Up at seven I felt almost too done in to face the final day, wanting to stay in bed till it was time for the plane to leave, but Margarita met us at half past nine with a British Council car, to show us around the Kremlin which we hadn't been inside before.

Long queues at the gate soon dissolved, and rain stopped for a while. We joined straggling bands of tourists by the Great Cannon manufactured in 1595, but never fired. Maybe it would have blown itself and too many bystanders to pieces. Half a dozen cathedrals came next but after the third it was hard to remember what I had already seen, so smothered were their walls with icons. The next interesting place was the Archbishops' Palace, with numerous glass cases of silver and gold artefacts.

A couple of hours to see so many wonders could only be a reconnaissance. One needed a week, maybe more, and I was too tired to take in the overwhelming detail. The eyes shivered back into their sockets at such dazzling objects. Outside, between the cathedrals, a score or so of children stood in a tight colourful circle that, from a helicopter, would have looked like a picturesque football supporter's rosette.

The drive to the airport was slow, due to traffic and poor visibility in rain and sleet. Margarita told us she had spent four years in Quito, where her father had been a diplomat. She had married a man from Ecuador who still lived there because of difficulties getting permission to be with her in Russia, but in a few weeks she would be going back to Quito to try and sort matters out. We wished her luck, and kissed her goodbye.

At the airport a militiaman by the anti-terrorist checkpoint noticed that we didn't have the obligatory labels on our hand luggage. They should have been stuck on at the BA checking-in desk, so we backtracked through the system to get it done. We took off our shoes to pass between the Scylla and Charybdis of the radar beams. Warning blips usually sounded for the Morse key and oscillator but, strangely this time, they didn't register as potentially suspect.

Sadly, the last thing I read in *The Moscow Times* was an item about a fire which almost gutted a synagogue on the outskirts of the city. The cause of the conflagration was not immediately clear. Firefighters had rushed to the blaze but were unable to prevent severe damage to the interior and the roof.

At the duty free we bought two bottles of Standart vodka, having been advised it was the best. After a long wait we boarded the large Boeing and set off for London. With the time change we arrived at six-thirty local time and, once out of the customs, spotted the pre-booked taxi driver.

A week or so later we heard with much sorrow that George Andjaparidze had died during the operation. He had been born in a German air raid, to the sound of falling bombs, and bursting shells from thousands of anti-aircraft guns defending the people of Moscow. Under the loving care of his mother and his aunt he was a fat and bonny baby, so well fed in times of terrible shortages – he never knew how they had managed it, because many other children had died – that he was nicknamed by them 'Our Little Bomb'. The two devoted women spoiled him, and perhaps partly for that reason he grew up to be amiable and tolerant, always ready and able to enjoy himself.

I'd had the privilege of knowing him as a friend, and several times saw how popular he could be with others, such traits lasting all his life. He implied, on our last evening together in Moscow, that it had been easy for Kuznetsov to turn him into an acquaintance who would stand by him.

He went on talking about Kuznetsov even after I had put my notebook down. 'The step he took was senseless, and I'll never stop thinking so. He must have realised that his money would soon run out, and who would employ someone who knew no English? Russian was the language in his blood, so who indeed would even remember him after a few years? Yet I had up to then seen him as a man with a head on his shoulders, sober and perhaps even calculating, but there are still so many puzzles in the affair that no matter how much I go over every little detail of the case I can't, even now, understand why he did such a thing, though a few clues and some information have come to me since.

'I was often asked,' he went on, 'why I didn't stay in England when I so easily could have done. I liked England very much, and still do. It's a wonderful country. Just imagine, I would have become a professor of Russian literature, and had a well-paid post in some university. I would have had it made, as you say.

'Yet thank God I didn't stay, because if I had I would have felt guilty and miserable for ever, which in a way means I'd have been ruined too. And I didn't stay because I loved my beautiful unfortunate nation more. It would have been a betrayal of trust, and I was never a treacherous person. My relations with the KGB afterwards were good because I kept absolutely nothing at all back of my experiences in London. I was never afraid of the KGB, though on one level after coming home it took a long time to become my normal self again. I was shellshocked, as you can imagine.

'In the end, though, I still can't understand why Kuznetsov did as he did. A question that still nags me is why, on his defection, he didn't go straightaway on the radio and television and say why he had done it. Instead, a whole fortnight went by before he went on the radio to denounce his country. Perhaps he did want to do so immediately, but was either advised not to, or was prevented.

'More mysterious was the fact that I was due to leave for Moscow a full three days before him, because I had important appointments to keep. I received permission to go, which would have given Kuznetsov three days in which to wander on his own. So why didn't he wait till then and defect, which would have been more certain and sensible? He wouldn't have betrayed my trust, though I realise now that might not have weighed very heavily with him, unless he had been told to do it when he did because those who helped him wanted to draw me as well into the net of defection.

'Another thing I remembered in my report was that not long after we had arrived in London he went into a booth and made a telephone call, which must have been to someone who spoke Russian and who he'd already been in contact with. Now, the

242 of Gadfly in Russia

mechanism of making such a call in London is different to what you do in Moscow, so who taught him how to do it? Or trained him?

'I didn't think anything of it while making the report, but about ten years ago someone who went through the archives found out that Kuznetsov had been a KGB agent. That explains the telegram which came to the embassy demanding that they get him back "at any cost". To have a writer run away was one thing, and I don't suppose all that unusual, but an agent is a much bigger fish, and no doubt he had much to inform the Foreign Office about in London.

'Such a fact only brings up more questions, which I suppose will never be answered, unless one day someone in your democratic country is given the liberty to go through the archives of MI5 or whatever it's called. I would dearly like to know.

'In spite of all that happened to me as a result of that affair,' he said finally, 'I've been a happy man. My only bitterness is that the trouble I was in had such a terrible effect on my mother that she died much sooner than she should have done. It did, literally, drive her to the grave, because she knew that in Stalinist times, which she had lived through, I would have been shot – no question. Now let's have a last drink together.'